TRIGG
The voice of mental health

The**inspirational**series™
Overcoming adversity and thriving

Stripped Bare
Swapping Credit for Compassion

BY SHARON BULL

We are proud to introduce The**inspirational**series™. Part of the Trigger family of innovative mental health books, The**inspirational**series™ tells the stories of the people who have battled and beaten mental health issues. For more information visit: www.triggerpublishing.com

THE AUTHOR

Sharon works as a speaker / writer through her business A Compassionate Voice, helping others through her own experiences with mental illness, recovery and wellbeing.

Sparking interest from the regional and national media, her story has appeared in *Woman's Own*, *Psychologies* magazine, *Stella* magazine and others. Her debut TV appearance was on *This Morning* in 2017.

Sharon has written articles for *Action for Happiness*, *The Wildlife Trust*, and *Everyday Mindfulness*, amongst others. She is a blogger for *The Huffington Post*, writing about mental health and animal welfare.

Sharon's speaker packages are a huge success at mental health seminars, wellbeing exhibitions, and animal welfare events.

First published in Great Britain 2018 by Trigger

Trigger is a trading style of Shaw Callaghan Ltd & Shaw Callaghan 23 USA, INC.

The Foundation Centre

Navigation House, 48 Millgate, Newark

Nottinghamshire NG24 4TS UK

www.triggerpublishing.com

Copyright © Sharon Bull 2018

British Library Cataloguing in Publication Data

A CIP catalogue record for this book is available upon request
from the British Library

ISBN: 978-1-912478-54-5

This book is also available in the following e-Book formats:

MOBI: 978-1-912478-57-6
EPUB: 978-1-912478-55-2
PDF: 978-1-912478-56-9
AUDIO: 978-1-912478-82-8

Sharon Bull has asserted her right under the Copyright,
Design and Patents Act 1988 to be identified as the author of this work

Cover design and typeset by Fusion Graphic Design Ltd

Printed and bound in Great Britain by Clays Ltd, Elcograf S.p.A.

Paper from responsible sources

www.triggerpublishing.com

Thank you for purchasing this book.
You are making an incredible difference.

Proceeds from all Trigger books go directly to
The Shaw Mind Foundation, a global charity that focuses
entirely on mental health. To find out more about
The Shaw Mind Foundation visit,
www.shawmindfoundation.org

MISSION STATEMENT

Our goal is to make help and support available for every
single person in society, from all walks of life.
We will never stop offering hope. These are our promises.

Trigger and The Shaw Mind Foundation

Creating hope for children,
adults and families

In loving memory of Kevin Anthony Bull
(25th Oct 1932 – 12th November 2003)

A doting father and best friend, and forever my hero! XX

Disclaimer: Some names and identifying details have been changed to protect the privacy of individuals.

Trigger encourages diversity and different viewpoints, and is dedicated to telling genuine stories of people's experiences of mental health issues. However, all views, thoughts, and opinions expressed in this book are the author's own, and are not necessarily representative of Trigger as an organisation.

INTRODUCTION

In 2010, I was finally forced into evaluating my life. I had no alternative.

For over 14 years, I had been living the dream – or so it seemed to my family, friends, colleagues, business clients, and neighbours. Passers-by might have taken my appearance at face value and automatically thought, *Wow, it looks like she's got it good!*

And yet the truth is, it was an extremely difficult time for me. After a shock redundancy in March 2010, my life as I knew it was turned completely upside down. I lost almost everything, coming close to taking my own life in a suicide attempt.

Over the years, working as a successful sales executive, I had grown accustomed to all the financial trappings that accompanied the job. As I handed back the keys for my company car, I knew the salary and bonuses had come to an end too. Gone also were the fancy holidays, my wardrobe full of designer clothes and shoes, and consequently my self-respect, because I placed all this material stuff above everything else.

But it's in adverse times we grow and learn, even though we don't see it at the time.

In a book called *How to be Compassionate*, by the Dalai Lama, he says, "'In my own life, the most difficult periods have been the times when I have gained the most knowledge and experience." I can relate so much to these words. The Dalai Lama's wisdom encouraged me to reflect on the difficult times in a more positive way. I say I lost almost everything, but what remained –

after being stripped of all the superficial garbage that I believed for 30 years to be the key to all happiness – was *me*. My true, authentic self.

It's hard to believe now that my image and importance of my status within society had somehow become the focus of my life. Sadly, this self-centred obsession with cars, body image, money, and promotion affects so many of us, and it's galvanised by years of cleverly constructed marketing, engineered by banks and large corporate businesses to make huge profits.

What baffles me the most about this time in my life is that despite having everything I thought would make me happy, I couldn't see that I wasn't. My constant bouts of severe depression, anxiety, stress, low self-esteem, and debt were all painting a completely different picture. And it wasn't happiness!

Up until 2010 I was completely occupied by a self-cherishing attitude, a mentality that seems to be encouraged across western civilisations. We are persuaded by advertisers never to be satisfied with who we are and what we have. We are constantly striving to be better than the next person by improving our status, climbing the corporate ladder, and accumulating material possessions. But at what cost?

It is no surprise that there is a rise in mental illness. This is a sickness which has no boundaries or prejudice as it weaves its way into schools, workplaces, and other walks of life. It affects the rich and famous, the young and old, males and females, the poor and disadvantaged.

Just like every other living being on this planet, we enter this world with absolutely nothing. And no matter how much wealth we accumulate during our tiny spell here, it is worth remembering that we still leave in the same way we arrived – with absolutely nothing.

I look back on my 14 years in a sales career and realise I was never actually cut out to be the aggressive hard-sell negotiator. But I'd strived for such a long time to be in this type of post. I saw it as a glamorous role, one with a multitude of perks and a high salary. What I didn't foresee were the long days, hours stuck in motorway traffic, or the numerous times I got soaked in downpours as I trudged the streets, weighed down with sample goods.

And while I was trying to keep up appearances in my working life, my personal situation was becoming almost unbearable. My spending was spiralling out of control and creditors called me around the clock for missed payments. My shopping addiction was encroaching on other areas of my life, especially my financial wellbeing. It was crippling my bank account to the point where I couldn't even manage to make the monthly minimum payments on credit cards.

Rather than face the music, I buried my head in the sand, wallowing in self-pity. I couldn't seem to admit to myself the severity of the situation, preferring to stall creditors with excuses. I was just like a ticking time bomb waiting to go off, my stress levels were so high. Yet, my continued refusal to seek help because of shame was only exasperating the circumstances.

I do believe we are eventually sent warning calls from a higher power to divert us from paths that destroy our true spirit. Your warning call may be illness, redundancy, loss, or even a break-up in a relationship. And although this may seem totally unfair, a complete travesty, or an injustice at the time, it can – sometimes – be our saving grace. I look back over the years to consider the countless obstructions, hurdles, difficulties, drawbacks, and hindrances thrown across my path and wonder why my brain just didn't register the messages being sent. For 30 years I battled with mental health issues. From leaving school I had been plagued by low self-esteem, but it wasn't until I hit rock bottom that I began to evaluate my life. It suddenly became clear to me why I had a shopping addiction, and why I suffered from constant bouts of depression. I had never been comfortable with the character my ego was wanting me to portray.

Eventually, there was no escaping the mess I was in. But, unbeknown to me at the time, it was the turning point in my life.

I recaptured childhood passions and rekindled my love of nature, writing, and poetry, each becoming an aid to my recovery and wellbeing.

We live in a society fixated by status, competition, and consumerism. Through this type of thinking people can so easily become attached to a particular person, situation, or object, believing this will open the door to a more fulfilling and happier life. People want bigger houses, faster cars, promotions ... whatever external entity they think will bring them instantaneous happiness is merely a distraction, unless we are at peace with ourselves.

Competition isn't always a bad thing, but when it becomes an obsession driven solely by greed and power, it encourages a selfishness that has little or no respect for others. Corruption, bullying, and bestowing fear, pain or distress on any living being to achieve stature and material gain is certainly not the antidote to anyone's lack of wellbeing and happiness.

I owe my life to wildlife and nature, because after being stripped bare of all I valued materialistically, it was wildlife and nature that reopened my heart and reminded me who I truly was – a woman who, as a little girl, wouldn't shoo a pigeon, who spent most Sunday afternoons picnicking in the countryside. A woman who, even at the height of her hard-hitting career, still wouldn't tread on a spider.

I have loved animals since I was a little girl, yet I never really considered that I could possibly make a difference for them. Perhaps being heavily influenced by a possession-led mentality got in the way of my true values, or maybe I didn't feel they ranked high enough in my list of priorities. Whichever it is, I now ask myself why, when saving the life of a flea battling to survive in the bird bath, it is equally as important to me as caring for my 16-year-old cat Maddie.

For 30 years, the genuine Sharon Bull played second fiddle to all the absurd distractions I associated with being happy. And it wasn't until I reached my lowest point that I found what I believe to be my purpose. At first, I had no idea how I was going to turn things around, but now I am working as an inspirational speaker, author, and poet under my brand A Compassionate Voice. The sole purpose is to raise awareness, inspire, help, and give hope, using my own experiences with mental health issues. I also share the story of how my change of lifestyle and thought processes assisted my recovery. My experiences have shown me that just because it's always been one way, it doesn't mean it has to stay that way!

Encouraging others to overcome their personal hurdles, highlighting the impact of nature and wildlife on wellbeing, and enlightening people about countless animal welfare issues has enriched my life in ways I could never have imagined.

This book clearly proves that we can transform our own lives by listening to our hearts, and we can also encourage others to do the same. Firstly though, we must work hard at fulfilling our own personal happiness and wellbeing. I gave myself a complete lifestyle makeover, replacing bad habits with good habits. I wrote, exercised, and walked – particularly around nature – and took part in daily meditation and mindfulness practices. All of them filled the void that the shopping addiction left behind.

It hasn't been easy, but nothing is achieved by a quick fix. My success has come about through sheer determination, perseverance, and patience. Some days were much more difficult than others and I still slip up from time to time. But I have also learnt not to dwell, to forgive myself, learn from mistakes and press ahead with what's important.

We are all connected to nature and wildlife. Equally, though, we are all connected to each other. Therefore, having unity, compassion, and kindness is the only way we will ever see positive changes in the world. If I can make these changes, anyone can. So, although *Stripped Bare* tells my personal story, perhaps what you recognise within me is a part of you too!

CHAPTER 1

once upon a time

I don't think I liked myself very much as a child.

There are only a few snapshots of childhood memories flickering around in my mind, like long-forgotten pictures in a dusty old photo album. I do, however, remember feeling clumsy, awkward, and plain-looking most of the time. I looked up to my cousins and felt envious of school friends, especially the girls with long, flowing golden hair. Mum, like most mothers around the time of my childhood, kept my hair extremely short in her combat to keep the headlice away, and so I yearned to have my hair in a ponytail or plaits.

I was six years old when my infatuation with Marilyn Monroe started. I didn't dream about being a princess like most little girls; I just wanted to be like Norma Jean – a beautiful lady who had transformed herself into a Hollywood movie star. I loved her stylishly curled blonde hair, curvaceous body, and desirable clothes. I played wonderful make-believe games with Mum's personal belongings, tippy-toeing around the family home in her high heels. I would mimic Marilyn's hip-swaying walk and smudge on some of Mum's ruby-red lipstick.

To me, an impressionable child, Marilyn was the epitome of beauty and elegance. She appeared to have everything her heart desired. I wanted to look like her when I got older, wear a beauty spot on my lower cheek and wear the types of dresses she wore in *Gentleman Prefer Blondes*.

And yet, I began watching her movies four years after her death from a barbiturate overdose. She was only 36. It didn't occur to me as a little girl whether she was happy or not.

Now, after reading countless books about the film star, I know she wasn't truly happy – even though her well-documented glamorous lifestyle portrayed her as having the perfect life.

Life gave my parents a raw deal during our infancy. Being a small child, I didn't have any real concept of how tough the times were for Mum and Dad. My brother Paul, being two years younger, was probably even more oblivious to their plight. By the mid-sixties we had moved home on more than one occasion, and my parents struggled financially during those earlier years due to misfortune and ill health. Dad had been regularly incapacitated by illness, but they kept the other reason for their money constraints a well-hidden secret for years.

I am also curious as to whether their financial plight unknowingly left a negative impact on my tiny mind about wealth and stature. Please don't get me wrong, my brother and I were dearly loved and although our parents could rarely afford the best toys on the shelf, they always tried to make sure we never went without.

I attended a Catholic primary school, where I was inspired regularly by nuns. I became fascinated with the idea of a vocation within the Church. I was only nine at the time, so I've never been certain what the intrigue was. Perhaps it was the attire they wore, or a curiosity about the convent and the lifestyle they lived. Maybe I was influenced by our wonderful family babysitter, Bridget, who at that time was a novice nun preparing for her ordainment. One thing I am sure about, though, is that my aspiration to be part of something holy had nothing to do with the Church or the priests serving the parish at that time. I found them both extremely intimidating.

For many years I've told my *Sound of Music* story at parties, jokingly declaring that as an adult, the thought of wandering around quietly in a convent – adorned only in a habit and veil and not wearing any make-up – was just too hideous to even consider. 'How Do You Solve a Problem Like Maria?' would probably still be my anthem tune today, but were I to reconsider my decision to join a holy sisterhood meditation, flat shoes and make-up-free days wouldn't bother me any more.

To be perfectly honest, I was never encouraged by the Sunday sermons. My father was outgoing but humble with his religious commitments, and for that reason our family would sit towards the back of the church. From such a distance, I found it difficult to engage with what was happening at the altar, so I would spend most of my time either watching the clock or teasing my younger brother, Paul.

It was through this boredom and a natural inquisitiveness that I began to notice a divide between the wealthy and working class within the parish. It certainly left me with a bitter taste towards the Church for many years. My name for the wealthy was "the fancy hats brigade". I would watch the upper class of the congregation trip over each other's feet, fighting for the pews at the front of the church. The husband would walk down the aisle, parading his wife in her big floppy hat and dangling his keys to their flash BMW for everyone to see. Their perfect children would walk behind them, the girls in bonnets and lacy gloves, the boys suited and booted without a hair out of place.

When Mass finally came to an end and the organ played out its final few notes, the parish priest would always walk slowly down the church aisle, making his way towards the enormous porch entrance in order to greet his parishioners. Jumping out of their front-row pews to follow at his heels, the fancy hats brigade would shadow him closely. By the time Dad, Mum, Paul and I reached the church's huge wooden doors, we would barely be able to see the top of the Holy Father's head, let alone receive his handshake.

Even at such a tender age, I reckoned spending an hour in a holy place once a week didn't constitute goodness in a person. Nor did deep pockets entitle someone to an automatic first-class ticket to heaven. Even as a small child I was trying to figure out the difference in social class. One Sunday morning I grabbed hold of my dad's hand as we stepped outside the church.

'Dad, does having lots of money make it easier to get to heaven?' I asked him. Bewildered by some of the parish's behaviour, I must have been desperately trying to understand humanity's cravings for stature, importance and supremacy.

My dad's response was convincing enough for me. 'Sharon, the only sure way of obtaining a key to heaven's door is by always sharing your love and kindness with others.' Mum and Dad lavished me and Paul with heaps of the stuff, so in my eyes they certainly qualified as exceptionally good people.

I didn't think Jesus could be swayed or influenced by the vast amount of money in someone's bank account. I doubt he cared what brand of car a family used to drive to church either – if that was the case, our ten-year-old Ford Cortina would never have made the grade.

I left a Catholic education behind after choosing to become a nurse, rather than a nun. My 11-plus results allowed me to attend a secondary school dedicated to this caring profession. The all-girl school's Sixth-Form nurse training was highly recognised for its success, and I was so excited to begin my new journey.

Attending a non-Catholic school made it so much easier to turn my back on a religion I thought was steeped in bias, although sometimes at Christmas, Easter, and even the odd sunny Sunday morning, I would proudly join my devoted dad in his usual seat at the back of the church.

There were also other advantages that came with my new school. I was pardoned from religious studies because of my faith and was asked to concentrate on a chosen project during the class. I was slowly metamorphosing into a young woman.

I found an ear for pop music and an eye for the pop musicians delivering the great sounds. At the time, David Bowie was at the top of my list of idols, so I decided to base my project on Japan, his favourite country.

How I loved my religious studies class, which was more than could be said for the rest of the school's curriculum. My enthusiasm for learning was swiftly deteriorating, the only other subjects in which I had even a spark of interest were English and Cookery.

Another bonus was the distance from home to school. It was just a short stretch across my local park and past the swings, where I had started to meet up in the early evenings with some boys and girls who were around the same age as me.

One day I had just crossed the park with a couple of friends when we were joined at the school gates by some concerned classmates. They had heard a whisper that a renowned Fifth-Form bully was gunning for me and urged me to go straight into the safety of the school grounds. They told me not to go to the tuck shop as usual, because they knew this was where the bully was waiting for me.

I was barely out of my first year, but she seemed to love making younger students cry. Whether it was brave or stupid, I ignored their advice and made my way to the tuck shop – I didn't want to be seen as a coward.

But as I approached her crowd of admirers, I was shaking with fear. The bully strutted like a peacock at the centre of her fan club, who were egging her on to deal the blow. My friends pleaded with me to turn around and run back to the school, but by then it was too late – my name was finally added to her scoresheet. She punched me hard in the face, but it wasn't so much the stinging on my cheeks from her fist that caused my tears to fall. It was the embarrassment of it being witnessed by so many schoolkids.

My appearance was starting to become massively important to me. The summer school uniform was a straight up and down patterned shift dress, which fell unfashionably to the knee. I remember, one morning, trying every which way possible to hitch up my school dress just a little. I finally hooked up with the idea that a belt around my waist would resolve the problem.

Success! I looked at my reflection delightedly in the mirror, admiring the outcome. The dress was now an inch above my knees, and the black shiny PVC belt – which sat perfectly around my midriff – added an edge of coolness. I couldn't see where I was breaking any rules within the school's dress code, but that day I got my first reprimand – the first of a few.

My detentions and telling-offs were mainly due to harmless schoolgirl pranks. In my third year, I encouraged the whole class to hide by the school gym. We could see our classroom from that viewpoint. It was hilarious to watch the teacher's face, when he thought no one had turned up for registration.

I wasn't unintelligent, but at the time I seemed to have made my mind up that I didn't need to learn. Instead, I preferred having fun. University wasn't an option because my parents just couldn't afford it. And my intention to stay on into the Sixth-Form to start nurse training was quashed when I realised I couldn't stand the sight of blood!

It wasn't easy for my parents. Mum had been forced back into a full-time job, because although Dad was still in employment, his arthritis was becoming more severe. It didn't take a rocket scientist to realise that it wouldn't be long before he was asked to leave. His sick days were fast outnumbering the days he was able to work.

My brother and I were both capable of getting to and from school, but I do feel like I let them down considerably during my latter years in education. My character seemed to change, and I favoured boys, cigarettes, and cider over homework, career planning, and exams. Although my school was an all-girls one, it didn't seem to hinder our chances with the boys. Quite the opposite! There was never a shortage of admirers from the two neighbouring mixed schools standing outside the gates.

After months practising with a settee cushion, I had my first kiss at a joint 14th birthday party for me and my friend. An older local boy caught my attention during the get-together, and somehow our teenage fumble took place underneath a piano in the hired room. For a number of weeks afterwards I was constantly teased by my chums. But it didn't matter – I secretly enjoyed the attention.

Ashamedly, the tables were turned during my final year and I became a Fifth-Form bully myself. I never dished out any blows – violence wasn't my scene – but psychological intimidation is equally soul destroying. A few of us would write anonymous nasty letters to girls in lower years, particularly the pretty ones. I'm not sure where my head was at that point. I don't know whether I was trying to cover up three years of mediocre exam results with a couldn't-care-less attitude, or if the bullying was masking my own low self-esteem. I had let the education system slip through my fingers, shifting my focus from finding the perfect vocation to finding the perfect man. Maybe I was lashing out, disillusioned with myself – realising just a little too late that my lack of attention to study was going to cost me dearly. Whatever it was, I am definitely not proud of some of my actions during those last days of school.

At 15 I hit the bottle. Not the whisky bottle, the peroxide bottle. Mum had always made it perfectly clear that until I left school, bleaching my hair was against the rules. But rules were meant to be broken. So, with some money put aside from my weekend waitressing job, I sneakily bought the inexpensive do-it-yourself kit.

The end result was a disaster. My hair turned a bright canary yellow, not the white-blonde colour I was hoping for. It certainly wasn't the best look. Mum's face was a picture when she walked through the living-room door.

'My God, Sharon, what have you done?' She looked at my hair in both disbelief and horror. My parents had been out for a couple of hours that evening with friends, giving plenty of time for the colourant to take effect. 'That's what you get for buying cheap hair products behind my back!' Mum's hair was her pride and joy. It was a beautiful white blonde, which she either held in a bun or tied up neatly in a ponytail.

'I just wanted it to look like yours,' was the only response I could give.

Mum knew the damage was done and there was little she could do, other than improve the situation. Luckily, my cousin Sandy was a professional hairdresser with her own salon, so she booked an emergency appointment for me. Sandy restored my hair to a more natural blonde colour, and my new grown-up look was here to stay.

I was 16 when I walked through the school gates for the last time. I knew there was a job waiting for me as a shop assistant in a local convenience store and, although it didn't pay much, it would mean a weekly wage packet. I passed the interview with flying colours, even though I'd climbed the stairs to the shop owner's office trembling like a leaf. His small workforce had painted a very worrying picture about their boss in the few minutes I waited for his call. They huddled around me at the back of the meat counter, gossiping about his tendency to chat up younger female staff and his lengthy lunch-time sessions in the pub, which very often stretched way after shop closing time.

I'd had a few weekend jobs during school, but this was my first taste of real independence. It was also the beginning of an extremely testing time for me, because almost instantly after leaving school, I began struggling with my identity. I became completely disillusioned with who I was and totally confused about what I wanted from life.

CHAPTER 2

no man will marry you

I climbed the stairs to the shop owner's office. It was my first day and I had been summoned by the boss. Mr Morris wanted to see his new starter.

It was mid-morning and the hot summer sun was starting to kick in. Mr Morris's office door was flung wide open, but judging by his appearance it wasn't having any effect on the sticky, warm atmosphere. His office was towards the back of a large storage area, which also doubled up as a staff canteen. There were a couple of chairs, an old kettle and an ashtray for the smokers. It wasn't very pleasant, being dimly lit, but it became a sanctuary for me during those first few days. There I could enjoy a cigarette and eat the packed lunch Mum had made up for me.

I tapped gently on the open door. Mr Morris beckoned me in, pointing to the empty chair in front of him. I timidly approached the chair, noticing the beads of sweat on his forehead. His shirt was unbuttoned almost to his navel, exposing an extremely hairy chest and a large, gold-coloured medallion hanging from a chain around his neck.

I was very uncomfortable. In my first few hours as his employee, I had heard so many stories about his supposed philandering.

'How are you settling in, Sharon?' That wasn't too intrusive a question to ask a new employee. His second question, though, seemed to take a quantum leap into the murky world of perversion. 'Are you on the pill?'

Having already been warned that he would ask this question, I wasn't thrown off balance. I was 16, fresh out of school and feeling extremely vulnerable, but I was adamant I wasn't going to be intimidated into doing anything I didn't want to do. I answered with a determined 'No.'

He then invited me to lunch. This made me nervous. I knew I could possibly lose my job if I answered too abruptly, so I made an apologetic excuse to him about Mum's packed lunch and it seemed to do the trick.

Thankfully Mr Morris never really bothered me again, and during my short spell at the convenience store, I even managed to get promoted to the till. Mr Morris had been impressed that I'd managed to uncover some shoplifters. They turned out to be regular customers who'd realised that Mr Morris had taken his eye off the ball, preferring to be in the pub instead.

Soon it become clear to me that the theft in the shop also extended to some of the staff, which is when I knew I had to get out. I left for a new job at a local factory and read in the regional paper that the business had collapsed a short while afterwards. I wasn't surprised; the unopened red letters were already stacked high on Mr Morris's desk before I left. The writing was on the wall.

My new job at the factory could be quite tedious. Packing drinking glasses into fancy boxes for the retail shelves didn't need high levels of intelligence, but the wages were higher. I made some good friends, including my best mate Marie, and my weekly pay packet matched my lifestyle better. Just like most 17-year-old girls, nights out with workmates, new clothes and make-up all became normal expenses for me.

For the next couple of years, I lived my life like most teenagers. It was the late seventies, the era of boogie nights, discotheques, the sounds of ABBA, and the emergence of punk rock into the UK's pop music charts. Sometimes at night, Dad would be waiting on the doorstep when I got home because I had dared to pass the 11pm curfew by a few minutes. He wasn't strict – quite the opposite, really. He was just a doting father doing his best to keep his daughter on the straight and narrow. And my choice of boyfriends often worried my parents. They tended not to be the settling-down type, despite my feeling that the only way out of my humdrum working existence was to become a wife and mother.

Beneath the surface, I had this underlying, growing frustration with life. I can only describe it as a continual itch that I couldn't seem to scratch.

It was the 8th March 1978, just after my 18th birthday, when a new wave / pop band named Squeeze made an unexpected impact on my life, tearing up the script I had written for myself. Finally, I was distracted from my endless pursuit of finding the perfect partner and marriage! Instead I found exciting new adventures. My love of live music was growing, and I preferred to pogo dance with an excited crowd at a concert, rather than swing my hips on a disco dance floor.

From the moment Squeeze walked onto the stage, I was completely blown away. My brother and I had bought tickets to see the show's headliners Eddie and The Hot Rods, and it wasn't often I could be bothered to watch any of the support acts. But for some reason this particular night was different. The lead singer had a towel over his head and mischievously played with the neck of his guitar. Cigar smoke billowed out from behind the keyboards. I don't know what drew me to the band, but something definitely struck a chord with me.

The next few years of my life took a surprising detour. Squeeze posters hung proudly from my bedroom walls, their tour dates became the most important days in my diary, and their singles and albums dominated my record collection. I planned my visits to their gigs with precision – once their dates were published in the music papers, I would instantly tick against the ones I could attend, put a cross beside the few I couldn't, and put a question mark next to any I was unsure of. I travelled the length and breadth of the country to see their gigs.

Most of my free time was influenced by my support for the band. I didn't just get a buzz from their shows. I loved the adventures – visiting new places, staying in hotels, hanging out with professional musicians. It all helped to drown out the boredom of my working life.

There was a big world out there, and it needed to be explored. It was far more exciting than looking for husband material. Settling down with a couple of children suddenly didn't seem so appealing any more.

And yet it was between the concerts and VIP backstage visits when I began to have problems. The ongoing, underlying frustrations I had with my life intensified until, without any warning, a severe bout of mental illness descended on me.

My mind was confused, frazzled – utter chaos. I was crippled by low self-esteem, disillusioned with my work situation, worried about my future, and suffocated by my own lack of ingenuity and talent.

The depression seemed to come from nowhere and with it came side effects such as panic attacks, heart palpitations, breathlessness, and severe headaches. These symptoms brought about a huge problem too, as I became extremely paranoid about my physical health. Some of my experiences were so harrowing, I remember them perfectly to this day.

One incident occurred when I was taking my usual route home from work. I began climbing the steep hill and had almost reached halfway point when I started to feel breathless. In what must have been a few seconds, the breathlessness escalated into a full-blown panic attack. I desperately flung my arms around a nearby lamppost, convinced I was about to die of a heart attack. Trembling, I crouched down onto the pavement, my back propped up against someone's garden wall. I listened to my heart racing; it seemed to be beating loudly and irregularly.

For quite some time I was scared rigid, unable to carry on climbing. The street was empty and there was no one to help me, so eventually I was forced into finishing my journey home.

A number of times I had to run out of shops, cafés, and pubs in a moment's notice – or get off a bus a few stops early – because of claustrophobia. My family and friends were continually taken by surprise with my irrational behaviour.

I had another panic attack while my parents were out one evening. Once again, my shortness of breath, heart palpitations, nausea, and trembling spiralled out of control. The scary symptoms gripped me with such intensity that I finally tried to find some solace by crouching down in the corner of the living room. I cocooned myself, wrapping my hands around my knees, and stayed there until my parents came home. Up until this point Mum and Dad had assumed I was suffering from a spell of teenage blues, but when they came home to find me cowering like a frightened child, they realised there had to be something much more sinister going on.

Mum made me an appointment with the family doctor. I found it extremely hard to explain to the GP what was wrong with me. At that point I don't think I even knew. I can't remember mental illness being openly discussed when I was young. After a couple of visits, I was diagnosed with an acute form of depression and referred to a psychiatrist.

I went to a number of appointments at the psychiatric unit, and usually one of my parents came with me. But one day neither of them could make it, so I took a friend. There was no reason to think that this meeting with my psychiatrist would be any different to previous visits – I'd always had the same trainee doctor. Maybe she was still learning the ropes, but she was lovely and seemed to understand exactly how I was feeling.

But I was in for a shock, as that morning she'd been replaced by the head of the department. He had a grey bushy beard, and he looked at me over his spectacles which were perched on the end of his nose. He had the look of an old, studious professor.

I soon realised that my consultation with him was going to be a lot less empathic and incredibly uncomfortable.

I honestly believe that this is when I formulated some extremely false perceptions about myself, which became embedded deeply into my psyche. They not only caused serious low self-esteem, but they also misguided my decision making and helped to draft out the next 30 years of my life.

'No man will marry you looking like that,' he said. 'Men don't marry women like you!'

I was humiliated. My eyes stung as tears slowly trickled down my cheeks, leaving trails of black mascara down my perfectly made-up face. I couldn't believe what I was hearing. This man was the head of the psychiatric unit – someone in a medical position qualified to help me in my time of need.

His voice sounded so remote, like he was talking to me from another room.

'How does your mum feel about the way you look?' he continued. 'Maybe you could seek advice from the ladies fronting the cosmetic houses in chemists and department stores?'

I said nothing. I cried harder and, feeling embarrassed at my vulnerability, bowed my head in shame. I watched as the teardrops fell onto my lap, turning my blue denim jeans a shade darker in colour.

My mood suddenly changed and I felt an instant urge to stand up and scream. My distress and embarrassment had turned to anger. I kicked my chair away violently, wiping away the remaining tears from my cheeks with the sleeve of my red fluffy jumper. Now the only things between us were his notepad and a half-filled mug of coffee.

He looked up at me, puzzled. This rather plump yet distinguished looking gentleman – whose eyes constantly seemed to be interrogating me over the rim of his spectacles – didn't seem to understand why I was so upset. I moved in a little closer, noticing the large, shiny gold buckle that was desperately trying to make an appearance between his white shirt and trouser waistband. The remainder of the leather belt was presumably hidden beneath layers of excess fat around his midriff. Numerous half-opened packets of biscuits lined the shelf behind him.

As he casually rested his arms across the dark wooden desk, I exploded.

'How dare you talk about me or my mum in such a way!' I yelled. 'Who are you to tell me how I should look or dress? And precisely *what* has this got to do with my illness?'

I began to shake as my rage reached a tipping point. I quickly picked up my belongings and, without waiting for his response, flew out of his surgery and back into the waiting room. Tears welled up in my eyes once again as I wrestled awkwardly with my coat, battling to pull my left arm through the sleeve while at the same time trying to zip up the main compartment of my handbag.

My friend Deborah was sitting and waiting patiently for my appointment to finish. I called out her name and she looked up from her lady's fashion magazine in utter disbelief. There I was, looking an absolute mess. I was standing bedraggled with just my right hand in the sleeve of my coat, the contents of my handbag strewn all across the floor and my red face covered in make-up streak lines.

How could I have possibly allowed this man to make me feel so bad, just because I didn't fit into his limited perception of the female role in society?

There was no doubt my appearance was a little eccentric. I stood out in a crowd, with curled, lacquered, bleached blonde hair and a perfectly placed beauty spot resting on my cheekbone. It was also no coincidence that the way I looked was heavily inspired by my childhood icon Marilyn Monroe. While my parents cringed at many of the outfits I chose to wear, they barely ever got in my way. I wore oversized coats, the shortest miniskirts, six-inch platforms and blood-red lipstick – and no matter how much my image embarrassed them, they realised that how I wished to express myself was my choice and not theirs.

'My God, Sharon. You look awful,' said my friend, shocked. 'What's happened? I thought you were here to be helped!' She dropped the magazine, galloped over to me and picked up the contents of my handbag from the floor.

I couldn't bring myself to discuss with her what had happened. My mind was racing, spinning. The humiliation, depression, and psychological pain was excruciating. All I wanted to do was run away, run outside into the main road – preferably in front of a bus. I wanted to find a place where no one knew me, somewhere I wouldn't be judged, a place where nothing mattered any more. I wanted to go somewhere I could simply be myself without any disapproval.

Looking back now, I will always be eternally grateful for Deborah's company that day, because if I had been on my own, I doubt I would still be here to tell the tale.

It still continues to puzzle me why the psychiatrist acted in such an insensitive manner. Was it merely the way mental illness was addressed by some of the medics at that time? Was it his way of getting me to "pull myself together"? Did he honestly think that his rude observations would destroy the low opinion I already had of myself?

I doubt I will ever be able to understand his motives, but I was absolutely determined to prove that the psychiatrist's theory was based purely on his own personal bias. I also vowed never to return to a clinic again.

Later that day, over our teatime meal, I managed to convince Mum and Dad that I had been given a clean bill of health and was therefore discharged from the clinic. They had already been through too much with my illness, so the relief on their faces when I told them this fabricated story confirmed to me that neither of them needed to know the reality.

CHAPTER 3

the next 30 years

Looking back at the 30 years leading up to 2010 is quite scary. It's sometimes hard to believe where the time has gone. I was a disoriented young woman beset – yet in some ways encouraged – by the words of a misguided psychiatrist. I was thwarted by the man's ridiculous notions of how a woman should behave, how she should look and what role she should play in society. Subconsciously I replayed his cutting words over and over again in my mind, and consequently I allowed his personal theories to be the dominating factor behind every decision I made.

I also recognise now that, over these 30 years, I was never emotionally equipped or strong enough to overcome my mental health issues alone. I tried to convince myself – after my disastrous and final encounter with the psychiatrist – that I could resolve my illness without any interventional help from medics, family, or friends. I suffered the consequences of my beliefs.

Happiness was always short-lived. Every opportunity was tainted because I undervalued my capabilities, my looks, and my importance to others. I would constantly take two steps forward and three steps back in all areas of my life. My romantic relationships were hindered, and although I pushed hard to succeed in my career, I was often my own worst enemy.

Depression constantly sat on my shoulders, waiting for the perfect opportunity to swoop down and envelop me. Just like any unwanted guest, the illness was a tireless intrusion. It came without any warning and was extremely difficult to shake off. I thought of the condition as a thief turning up unannounced, stealing my confidence, joy, laughter, and love.

One thing I am certain of, though, is this: while the psychiatrist's ill-chosen words accelerated my depression, it was also largely fuelled by my ego. My actions were governed by my critical self; I constantly sought approval because I needed to feel special. No matter what I achieved, I always told myself I wasn't good enough.

I remoulded my life after that psychiatric appointment, and the factory was my first platform. I took the first scary steps towards turning my dead-end job into a career. For the next 14 years I worked my way up through the ranks, brushing aside any advice from people whose motives I believed weren't entirely for my benefit. It was a lengthy, rocky road. I moved up from a packing job and started supervising the company's distribution, and then moved on again. I finally got my own desk in the marketing department. I faced a lot of handicaps and disappointments, but I can see now that these challenges shaped me into the person I am today.

It was during my short spell on the factory floor that I met my best mate Marie.

For a short while we lived together in a rented flat above some Relate marriage guidance offices. The rickety wooden staircase looked like the steps leading from the lower cabin of a boat onto its deck – and these were the flat's best feature! The two bedrooms were on the ground floor alongside the kitchen and bathroom, overlooking an extremely busy town centre road. Our sleep was interrupted most evenings by traffic noise or police incidents, so it wasn't long before we moved out and into a nicer place. This time it was a two-bedroomed house, complete with garden and stone ornamental bird bath. It was barely visible when we first moved in because the lawn was so overgrown!

While I enjoyed living with Marie, things became difficult very quickly. Jealousy and envy are widespread within corporate organisations, especially when competition and rivalry are encouraged. As I climbed the ranks from the factory floor into the despatch office, some of the department's long-term staff hated that I'd been promoted ahead of them. They were peeved that they had been overlooked by someone younger. Worse still, I was merely a factory girl. I couldn't possibly match their intelligence. Feeling angry and venomous, they used gossip and spite to try to damage my reputation. One or two even refused to acknowledge me as a supervisor. They'd create silly, petty incidences to knock my confidence.

Their constant attacks and attempts to ruin my reputation didn't dent my work ethic. But they were seriously affecting my self-esteem. They had no intention of helping me achieve the company targets, but I needed to prove my worth in society. It was becoming more and more important to me. I did get a reprieve when working late into the evenings and weekends with my own three recruits.

Eventually their animosity started to create a toxic atmosphere. It started to screw up my mind. After my promotion from despatch administrator to despatch office supervisor I found out that the long-term staff were talking about it behind my back. They were convinced that my step-up was because of my "popularity with the senior management", rather than the hard work I had put in to successfully restructure the office systems. I'd had enough – this was the final straw.

I started to argue with myself about my ability to succeed in a professional environment. My good results didn't seem to matter any more. And so, one day my erratic behaviour kicked in. Without any thought of the consequences, I stood up impulsively from behind my desk. It was time to take drastic measures.

Leaving several of my tasks unfinished, I grabbed my coat and handbag. I marched right out of the office and headed for my parent's home close by.

Dad couldn't believe it when I charged through the back door in floods of tears. But before I could explain myself, the phone's shrill ringtone cut into our conversation. I answered it and recognised the worried voice of the company's personnel manager. He had believed in me from the start and helped me build my career.

'Sharon, can you please make your way back to work and come to see me?' he asked. 'I can't do anything about the situation unless you do.'

At first I wasn't sure if I could be persuaded, but eventually I was convinced enough to go back. It didn't end well. Storming out had only fuelled the bitterness of the antagonistic few. Their resentment grew stronger, the hostility worse, and so my days in the job were numbered.

I couldn't handle the endless smear campaign any more, or the continual tittle-tattle. So many times I'd walk back into the office and be met with an uncomfortable silence. I knew they'd been talking and whispering about me. I could see guilt written across their faces as they scurried back to their desks.

Thankfully the nightmare was finally over when I was promoted into the marketing department. I was finally able to leave the malicious gossip behind me.

My end goal was to work in sales, preferably on the road as a sales executive. For me, this was the surest way to show the psychiatrist that I was the type of woman that men would want to marry. There was no doubt in my mind that this kind of career would lift my image, and I was sure that the money, clothes, and cars would make me much more attractive.

The Managing Director did quiz me about my motives. He was worried that I saw my new marketing job as nothing more than a stepping stone towards a sales career.

'What are the chances of my getting into the company's sales team?' I'd asked him a few months earlier, during his weekly visit to the despatch office.

His response wasn't particularly inspiring. 'I'm not sure there are any upcoming vacancies any time soon,' he said. He then went on to trample on any ideas I might have had about applying for external sales positions. 'Sharon, selling is a tough world. You either need experience or qualifications. Without either, your chances of getting a sales position elsewhere would be extremely slim.'

Maybe he was nervous about losing a conscientious member of staff. Perhaps he thought that, in sowing some seeds of doubt, he would kick the idea out of my head.

And he had every right to be worried – in 1994, having been in the marketing position for just over a year, I left the company. After 18 years of service, and now approaching my mid-thirties, I nervously handed in my notice to embark on my exciting new sales career.

For the first 18 months I worked as a team leader at a company called CPM, working with one of their major clients – a brand leader in confectionery. Supervising a team of eight merchandisers certainly had its perks! Apart from the endless chocolate sample supplies, their blue-chip sales and management training gave me the experience and the confidence I needed to move forward in my career.

Not long after I started this job, my dad suddenly fell terribly ill with an aortic aneurysm. And so, with my brother living in Norwich, I made the decision to move back home and help Mum with his care.

My new sales job offered me a brand-new company car and exciting bonus prospects, but I had taken a salary cut. It seemed a small price to pay for the experience and training within a blue-chip company, but paying my half of the bills and rent had started to become difficult. For this reason, I didn't need much persuading to give up my independence, and so Marie and I parted ways after a few years sharing food bills, pot washing and home parties.

My spending and borrowing was probably relatively normal at the time, but my desire to look good over the years had already made some deep impressions on my credit cards. I now needed to tighten my purse strings.

I also had an itch to earn a bigger salary. I trawled the pages of Grocer magazine, which was filled with job possibilities. Now that I had some blue-chip sales training, I assumed that I wouldn't have many problems with getting interviews. Besides, I wanted to buy my own house.

Dad was also feeling much better after recuperating from his life-threatening operation, so for the time being there was some normality back in our family lives. The job hunting process began.

As it turns out, I was right. It wasn't long before I made the switch from a team leader in a confectionery company to an Area Sales Manager selling travel accessories. With a bigger car, higher monthly income, and much more bonus potential, my model life was almost complete.

In 1997 I bought my dream home. All the banks were crying out for first-time buyers at the time, so 100% mortgages were really easy to get hold of. I only needed a small deposit, although it still baffles me how I managed to even scrape that together. Somehow, though, with my minuscule savings and a small loan from my parents, I pulled it off.

The bank was very quick to offer to help me, too. They gave me a loan against the house to buy furniture and white goods. Dad helped me turn the two-bedroomed semi-detached into a home fit for a female independent executive. In no time it was decorated in all my favourite colours, adorned with pictures and soft furnishings. I loved it.

My love life was almost non-existent, but I never gave up. I was a woman possessed, on a mission to prove that the psychiatrist's theories were wrong. I constantly searched for the "right man". As I moved up the career ladder, I looked for men who I thought were appropriate now that I was in my new sales role. I not only judged them by their appearance, but by their status too.

I'd had my first and last marriage proposal at the tender age of 18. I'd only been dating the boy eight weeks, so I quickly said no. And I can categorically say that since then, no one has truly loved me. I've been wined and dined, I've had men encourage my infatuation for them, and I've slept with some too – but none were supportive or a loyal friend.

I don't blame any of these men. I constantly set myself up to fail. I chased and grasped at potential partners. Some would run in the opposite direction after seeing the desperate look in my eyes; some would be flattered by the attention and abuse the situation.

Still, despite this, I had finally succeeded in getting everything I initially set out to achieve. I had a jet-set career and spent my days dressed in pencil skirts and matching jackets. With a briefcase in hand, newly learnt IT skills, great pay packets, and a company car, you'd think that I'd have been happy.

So why did it still feel as though there was something missing?

Throughout all this, the downs still outweighed the ups. For 30 years I had been continuously fighting, almost drowning in waves of highs and lows, often feeling dissatisfied with my life. I never truly learnt how to stay afloat during complicated setbacks, so my spells of happiness were short-lived.

'Why doesn't life feel as perfect as I dreamt it would be?' I couldn't stop asking myself this question.

The answer was simple; I just couldn't see it.

I never believed in myself, therefore I wasn't happy. It wouldn't have mattered how high I climbed up the corporate ladder, how big my house or car was, or how fancy my clothes were. None of it would ever have been good enough.

CHAPTER 4

the first sign

Just a couple of years into my role as a sales executive, I received my first warning call. Something in the universe tried to encourage me to change direction in life.

In high spirits one Friday morning, I was coming to the end of a two-hour journey from Derbyshire to Cheshire. I was driving along the last few miles of the M56 motorway.

I was on my way to visit a client in Chester, who had become a good friend of mine. I had met so many wonderful people since starting out with the company, which helped to make the untimely wake-up calls, long journeys and late nights much more bearable. (It certainly wasn't a nine-to-five job.) I'd never shied away from long hours, and this position gave me freedom to plan my days and the ability to work out the best strategies for meeting my targets. But I did learn quickly that the reality of a middle-class professional woman wasn't quite how I had envisaged it to be.

My expectations were based on the images I'd drawn up in my mind. I'd only thought about my standing in society and how I would look. I'd never considered the details of a sales executive's job description.

Thoughts of the shop manager's fresh coffee started to tickle my taste buds. I could almost smell the aroma of the coffee beans as I indicated and manoeuvred into the middle lane of the motorway. I pondered whether to give Marie a call later that day as I began to overtake a couple of vehicles driving steadily on the inside lane. We usually kick-started our weekend at a country pub called The Fox and Goose, but we still hadn't decided what to do. Now, the idea of a few glasses of wine to round up a particularly stressful week was very tempting.

The motorway was relatively quiet, which wasn't unusual for a Friday morning. I think a lot of travelling business people scheduled their diaries to stay local at the end of the week, or even worked from home. Considering the events that followed, I maybe should have done the same that day.

Everything was moving along fine – until a large chunk of metal fell from a lorry two vehicles ahead of me. When the driver of the small van in front saw the debris heading straight for his vehicle, he swerved erratically to avoid a collision.

The van clipped the runaway junk, which sent it hurtling straight into – and under – my car. Within the blink of an eye I lost control of my Toyota.

It all happened very quickly.

Suddenly my car seemed possessed, taken over by the devil. The scrap metal entangled itself with the undercarriage of the car, making horrendous and terrifying clattering noises. The whole vehicle shook violently. Frantically, and in a mad panic to regain control, I tightened my grip on the steering wheel while continually slamming my foot hard onto the brake pedal. But deep in the pit of my churning stomach I knew it was time to stop. There was nothing left that I could do.

What seemed like hours must have only been seconds, but I do remember feeling unexpectedly calm as I first released my foot from the brake pedal and then removed my hands from the steering wheel. I figured that whatever happened next was simply out of my control.

Looking back, I see it as a perfect example of letting go of a situation I had no power to change. I didn't know if I was going to die, be seriously injured, or come out of the accident totally unscathed, but I will always remember that after I made the decision to let it be, I no longer felt scared.

My last thought was, *don't think I will be going to The Fox and Goose this evening after all!* before the car raced across the motorway and hit a crash barrier on the hard shoulder.

I don't recall much about the final impact. The vehicle must have hit the barrier with such ferocity that it forced the car to spin around, so that the front end was facing the oncoming traffic. Queues started to build as the cars and lorries slowed down to get a look at the wreckage. Still in shock, I started to feel each of my body parts to make sure they were all intact.

I realise how lucky I was to emerge from the wrecked Toyota without a single blemish, but a lot of factors worked in my favour that day, and each of them helped to keep me alive. It happened on a Friday when the motorway was quiet, no other vehicles were travelling near me as my car hurtled across two lanes, and I now believe my relaxed state at the time of the smash protected me from serious injury too.

I was on the phone to Mum and Dad when both the front passenger and driver's doors flung open simultaneously. Two knights in shining armour suddenly peered into the car. I hadn't seen them pull up in their white vans. It's amazing that for months I'd cursed the infamous drivers of white vans for every infringement of the Highway Code. And yet here they were, the first to my rescue!

The pair immediately got into a squabble as they each gave me their conflicting instructions on what I should do, so it was quite comforting when the police arrived. I was still sitting in the car, feeling traumatised, when one of the officers held out his hand to help me out. 'Let's get you somewhere safe until the medics arrive to check you over,' he said to me kindly.

I did not expect to be sitting in the back of a police car taking a standard breathalyser test that Friday morning, but at least I was still in one piece. That was more than could be said for my car. It looked completely destroyed.

I refused to go with either of the two ambulances when they arrived on the scene. Instead, I asked if I could go with the Toyota and tow truck to the garage. My brother Paul, who was now living in Warrington decided to leave work and take me home. He collected me from the garage shortly after my arrival, but I don't think he was prepared for the extensive damage that had been done to the car.

'I can't believe how lucky you are to escape without any injuries,' he said incredulously, eyeing up the mangled car.

Dad encouraged me to get checked out at the hospital. To make sure I went, he offered to take me. After we left A&E we laughed heartily together at the unsightly neck brace I was made to wear while being forced to lay flat out on a trolley bed. It had been over 12 hours since the accident, but the hospital assured me they needed to take the necessary precautions for a neck or spinal injury. Thankfully I left A&E that evening with a fairly clean bill of health.

The Monday after the accident I was back behind the wheel of a car and working. My family were furious about the decision, but my thinking behind this was to banish any fears about driving following an accident. Besides, nothing – not even my health – was going to get in the way of my endless pursuit of success and stature.

I clearly didn't make the right judgement call, because a few months later I was seeing a specialist after being diagnosed with delayed trauma. And so it was that my decision never to see a psychiatrist again was thwarted.

I consoled myself with the notion that he was a counsellor, evaluating me on behalf of my insurance company's claim, which in my eyes was something completely different.

Jumping straight back into the saddle without seeking further medical advice caused repercussions that could have been avoided. My state of mind – which was delicate at the best of times – had been affected by the crash. Once again, I started suffering panic attacks. Flashbacks and sleepless nights became a regular occurrence.

After a few sessions with the counsellor, who talked me through the accident, assessed my emotions and gave me some coping measures to deal with the trauma, he reckoned there was no permanent mental health damage connected to the car crash. He reassured me that the flashbacks and nightmares would eventually become less and less frequent until they stopped completely.

I have always wanted to believe there is something or someone watching over us. Someone who knows more than we do, who understands why we are here and takes care of us until they know it is our time to go. On that spring morning in 1999, it definitely felt like there was an unexplained phenomenon with me in the car, sprinkling magic across my fateful path and cushioning me from harm. I believe it was the first warning sign that was meant to redirect me down another path.

But it was just one of several warning signs I chose to ignore over the next 10 years.

The next warning sign was just a few weeks after the counsellor had given me the all-clear. I had just started to feel that everything was back to normal when I felt an alien mass on my right bust for the first time.

Showering on a work day normally only took me two minutes because of time constraints. Nevertheless, I tended to use those precious moments to indulge with expensive skincare products. The warm water streamed from the showerhead and I allowed it to wash over me, basking in the delights of my new coconut-based shower cream.

And this was when I stumbled across the horribly large lump.

I froze like a robot. The water bounced off my forehead and my saturated hair fell over my eyes. I couldn't believe the bad luck I was having.

All I could do was keep feeling the tainted area, hoping against hope that I had made a mistake.

I don't know how long I stood there with the water spilling over me, but after a while I finally stepped onto the bathroom mat, feeling cold and shaky. I wrapped a warm towel around myself.

I felt sick, numb from shock. I didn't go to work and instead I headed straight to my parents for advice. If there were two people I could count on for support and comfort, it was Mum and Dad.

'Sharon, it's probably nothing. But let's get it checked out,' Dad said, trying to convince me there would be a positive outcome. Mum wrapped her arms around me as he tried to stay upbeat, but it was obvious they were both extremely worried.

We decided to make an appointment with the GP and I was referred to the hospital. It was an incredibly scary wait.

Marie and I had booked a long pamper weekend at a spa hotel near Stratford-upon-Avon; it had been pencilled in our diaries for quite some time. But it just happened that the hotel reservation was the weekend prior to my hospital appointment. The five-star accommodation was set within acres of fields, meadows, and forests. It was an idyllic getaway.

I just wasn't sure if I was in the mood for facials, body wraps, and pedicures.

Eventually Marie and my family persuaded me that going away for a few days would probably distract me from the stomach-churning worries I had about the lump's diagnosis. This couldn't have been further from the truth – even though Marie and I did share a few laughs (as best friends do), the words "breast

41

cancer" were never far away from my thoughts. In photographs I look back at myself posing and smiling among breath-taking views, and I can so easily see how worried I was. My mind was overwrought, tormented by the not knowing, the doubts, the possibilities of serious illness and life-changing consequences.

Thankfully the outcome was positive. I was immensely relieved. The screening showed a large benign cyst, and the doctors drained it quickly. I watched it on a monitor next to my bed.

I'd just turned 40 and was given a new chance at life. My whole life had raced through my mind in the shower that morning, as I contemplated everything I still wanted to do. I thought about what I hadn't yet accomplished, plans I hadn't carried out, and babies I still hoped to carry. The question of having children had badgered me for quite some time. I desperately wanted a baby.

While I sat with my doctor during the emergency appointment later that day, I quizzed her about her views on midlife motherhood. 'At what age do you think it becomes unsafe to carry a child?'

With no potential father even on the horizon, my chances of pregnancy were looking bleak. After my car accident and cancer scare, it almost seemed like time was running out.

Her answer? Forty-five.

I decided it was time to step up the search for Mr Right.

CHAPTER 5

150 miles away

It was Wednesday 12th November 2003, and it had been yet another exasperatingly busy working day in London. Each year around this time we launched a new collection at work from a luxurious hotel in the capital. With only two days left in our rigorous schedule, I had mischievously coerced Steve, one of the men in our team, to take me out that evening.

'Let's split the week up and have that night out we keep promising ourselves,' I suggested.

I had spotted a great play advertised in the West End. I reckoned a visit to the theatre – mixed with a little retail therapy and a bite to eat beforehand – was just the pick-me-up we both needed. Although part of a close-knit sales team, our friendship had developed into something special since I'd started out with the business in 1996. Most working days, Steve and I would call each other to check how things were. We were a sounding board for each other, musing over problems with clients, orders, or even management together.

'How about champagne in Selfridges too?' I asked excitedly. He didn't take much convincing. We'd been promising each other an evening out for a while now, so the thought of spending a few hours away from the bosses – whose conversations seemed to revolve purely around the following year's targets – couldn't have been more tempting.

I first noticed an advertisement for the play on the internet a few weeks before the exhibition. The actor in the lead role sparked my interest. I'd admired him for years, captivated by his beautiful blue eyes. I remember daydreaming about catching his attention from a front-row seat as he delivered his lines perfectly. He would whisk me off my feet, holding me tightly, and we'd have that one perfect kiss that would change my life completely.

It never occurred to me that he might be married. Finally finding true romance with someone who was not only extremely talented, but looked delicious too, was worth fantasising about.

I still hadn't found my Mr Right because I was probably looking in all the wrong places. I was being guided by my ego rather than my heart. I chased businessmen, musicians, and athletes. If I thought their lifestyles were exciting, I saw them as hot targets. My mind seemed to have a homing device, and it would deliberately seek out these types of men.

I fell desperately, obsessively in love more than once, but it wasn't always reciprocated. I was unknowingly controlled by this mental image of the perfect couple, living in the perfect house, enjoying the perfect lifestyle.

I purposely forgot to mention my obsession with the leading actor to Steve, and booked the tickets.

The company exhibition went on a lot longer than we'd expected, but although we were both tired, we were still determined to make the most of our evening together. With only a couple of hours to spare before the play, we stepped outside the hotel giggling and reminiscing about two very drunk customers, who'd stayed until the last bottle of wine was empty. They had placed a large order, though, so this made up for the copious amounts of wine and bubbly they'd drunk during the day.

The taxi pulled up outside Selfridges, and I felt an almost too familiar adrenaline rush sweep over me. I searched frantically inside my latest black designer handbag, pushing aside my hair lacquer, deodorant, and an assortment of perfume bottles. I reached for the Gucci purse I'd bought a few weeks earlier. With a sigh of relief, I quickly opened the card section, gently and reassuringly caressing my Visa cards with my thumb. Staring back at me was my exquisitely prestigious American Express card.

Plastic gave me an ability to spend lots of money. It triggered an excitement within me, one that made me feel extra special for a short while. I knew I'd been spending ridiculous amounts of money lately – far more than my salary could sustain – but somehow I just couldn't seem to stop splashing out. It didn't seem to register with me the terrible mess my finances were in. Maybe, deep down, I chose certain men because I saw them hopefully as resolutions to my mounting debt.

What I clearly wasn't doing was admitting that I had a serious problem with spending. Neither was I acknowledging that this pattern of behaviour was linked to addiction.

I walked into Selfridges with Steve by my side. The department store was simply oozing with glamour, stardom, and wealth. My six-inch heels, tight-fitted black dress, credit cards and faux fur jacket seemed to fit in perfectly.

We headed for the champagne bar. Steve and I were extremely good mates and we laughed loudly as we washed down aperitifs with a few glasses of Moët. The drink fuelled our giggling and it reached fever pitch.

It was so good to relax after such a hard day, but I needed to do some serious shopping before we headed to the theatre. I was desperate to see the Agent Provocateur lingerie department too. As I browsed through the beautifully displayed underwear, Steve's face was a picture. Still feeling the effects from the champagne and its bubbles, I teasingly held up an array of corsets and bras for his approval. Red faced with embarrassment, he eventually walked away. Pointing to his watch, he mouthed at me silently, 'You've got 10 minutes.'

The champagne had clearly gone straight to my head. Left alone to peruse the displays a little while longer, within seconds I was trying on two matching sets of lingerie in the changing rooms.

Why buy one set when there is enough plastic in my purse for two? I thought.

My mouth watered as I watched the shop assistant wrap the pieces of lingerie perfectly in soft tissue, before dropping them into a stylishly decorated box. Her make-up was flawless; her blushed cheekbones and ruby-red lipstick working perfectly next to her pearly white teeth. I handed over my American Express card and she beamed a radiant smile. 'Is there anything else we can tempt you with today, Madam?'

Hurriedly I scanned the department to check if there was something – anything – that would shout out at me and entice me to buy. But all I could see was Steve, who'd come back to collect me. He was standing at the edge of the department, vigorously pointing to his watch again.

I'm still not sure why I chose lingerie to buy that evening. There was still no man in my life to impress. I'm wondering if I ever read, in any of the numerous self-help books I had bought over the years, that true happiness, contentment, and confidence could only come from within. If I had, I clearly hadn't quite grasped the concept. I obviously thought that this straightforward message, helping me to find inner peace, was convoluted. The idea that wearing glamorous underwear would give me a dream life makes me realise how much mental work I needed to do.

The Agent Provocateur lingerie may have felt empowering underneath work suits and elegant party dresses, but apart from racking up another two hundred pounds on my next month's Visa bill, I doubt there was much else to be gained.

Steve must have realised that I had a secret fascination for the play's leading actor. He endured my continual drooling patiently each time the star looked out towards us from the stage. Obviously, my dream was merely a fantasy, but the night was perfect anyway. We enjoyed the play so much. Sitting in front-row seats meant that we could engage with the plot so much more. It felt like we were being drawn onto the stage and into the storyline.

Afterwards we decided to end the evening with a glass of wine in a bar next door to the theatre. It was the obvious choice, and not only to us. The pub was really busy. The only few empty seats were ridiculously high stools, and trying to get comfortable on one of them wearing a tight black dress and six-inch heels was almost impossible.

I had just managed to perch myself precariously next to Steve when I noticed the leading actor stroll past the window, clutching a garment carrier. I didn't waste any time. I leapt from my stool, pointing to the window, but I don't think Steve understood what was happening. Without waiting for his response, I ran out into the cold, dark London Street.

I couldn't see him at first, but then I noticed a familiar slim figure emerging from behind a standing taxi. I ran towards him as quickly as I possibly could in my high heels. He slammed the lid of the car boot shut and he turned around. There I was, a pen in one hand and a programme in the other.

'The play was amazing this evening,' I said to him, my heart pumping hard. 'Would you please sign my programme?'

My heart was racing fast, though that was probably down to the unexpected running rather than the excitement of meeting my idol. He looked great, standing tall in a long, cream-coloured raincoat. He signed his autograph on the front cover of the brochure. He was delightfully sweet, wishing me a pleasant evening and smiling as he handed back my pen.

I felt a little disappointed that nothing else happened. *Maybe he's not my knight in shining armour after all,* I thought.

But still I ran back into the pub like an excited child, waving the autographed programme for my bewildered friend to see.

'My God, Sharon. I was starting to wonder where you were,' he said, pushing the untouched glass of red wine towards me.

Before I could explain and show him the actor's signature, my mobile phone suddenly lit up on the pub table. I was still trying to clamber back onto the barstool when the unmistakable Madonna ringtone began to play.

I felt a jolt of sheer terror, and my excitement ebbed away. My brother's name appeared on screen as the caller.

Dad's health had deteriorated rapidly over the past year. He'd suffered a number of strokes, but his last one had been the most crippling, leaving him partially paralysed. But he had an unyielding will to survive, and he loathed being away from Mum, so after a while in a rehabilitating hospital, he'd been allowed home. Staff from different medical units planned coordinated home visits, and his quality of life had been improved just a little.

But now I automatically thought the worst. It was gone eleven o'clock, and there could be only one reason why Paul would be ringing me so late. I knew it wasn't good news.

'Oh, my God! It's my brother!' I blurted out. 'Please take the call for me, Steve. I don't think I want to hear this!'

Steve grabbed the phone from my hand and immediately accepted the call. Although my brother's voice was distant, I could still just about make out what he was saying.

'Please can you get a taxi to bring my sister home to Chesterfield immediately? Our father is dying.'

Those words still haunt me today.

Totally oblivious to the attention I was drawing, I began screaming loudly. Frantically pacing the floor, I bellowed, 'No, that can't happen. I'm not there with him!'

I was panic stricken, suddenly realising I was 150 miles away from home. 'I can't lose my best friend,' I sobbed.

Steve was still in conversation with Paul as I clumsily gathered together my things. Desperate to be back home with my family, I yelled at him to get off the phone.

Steve took complete charge of the situation. I will never be able to thank him enough for that. I think he could almost feel my anguish, so he wasted no time in hailing a taxi. London isn't the easiest place to get from A to B in a rush, but somehow the cab driver managed to get us back to the hotel fairly quickly. Steve never left my side. He helped me pack my suitcase and put me in a cab for the long drive home to Chesterfield.

How easily happiness can turn into despair! That evening was a perfect example.

The taxi driver must have had a difficult journey along the M1 to the Derbyshire market town, because unusually for me I didn't speak a single word. I have no memories of the man who drove those 150 miles in the early hours of a November Thursday morning. I have no idea what he looked like, how old he was, what nationality – nothing. As the car sped along an almost deserted motorway, I gazed out through the passenger window, mesmerised by the dancing night shadows and reflections created by distant lights, trees, and buildings. My mind drifted as I started to think about the rotten hand Dad had been dealt during his 71 years of life.

When he was in his early forties and I was midway through secondary school, he was forced into early retirement. He was a proud painter and decorator, and it almost crucified him. It was heartbreaking to realise that Dad's illnesses had finally won the battle, when he'd fought so hard to maintain the upper hand. Despite all this, though, he kept his dignity. And no matter how tough things got, he never let it affect his self-worth or optimism.

Despite having crippling rheumatoid arthritis, he accepted his fate and took on new challenges, including organising numerous charity events and raising lots of money for local causes. He probably would never have had the time if the circumstances had been different. He was a wonderful father and a perfect role model. He always declared that there were others far worse off than himself, even during his hardest days.

I couldn't help but smile through my grief when I remembered the last time he said it. We'd been to the football match together earlier in the afternoon, armed with our usual flask of tea and a bag of mixed sweets. We always enjoyed spending a few hours urging our local club to victory. Due to his illnesses, Dad often looked frail for his age, but he was in good spirits during the game.

Each match we would take turns driving to the game, and on this particular day it was my turn behind the wheel. I had just locked up for the evening after dropping him safely back home when the phone rang. Eager to change into my pyjamas, I was already halfway up the stairs. I thought about letting it ring.

'They'll leave a message or call back if it's urgent,' I mumbled to myself. But something inside me must have sensed the urgency, because my instincts told me not to ignore the call.

I ran back down the stairs and picked up the receiver. I heard my mum's worried voice on the other end of the line.

'Will you take your dad to the hospital, please, Sharon?' She sounded really frightened. 'Something's wrong. He needs to be checked over.'

'Yes, of course I will,' I told her. Without any hesitation I grabbed my coat, handbag, and car keys, and headed straight back to my parents' home.

Within the hour, Dad and I were walking through the automatic sliding doors into A&E. He turned to watch a young boy in a wheelchair pass by in the opposite direction. The little boy looked pale and thin. He was wearing a blue-and-white football hat, which I assumed was to cover the results of his chemotherapy. Smiling jovially, he waved at Dad, while a middle-aged man – probably his father – steered the chair out through the hospital doors. Close by their side was a smartly dressed blonde lady. Encouraged by the little boy's enthusiasm, she also looked at Dad and courageously raised a smile too. It was obvious she was struggling to keep up the pretence, but my dad waved back kindly.

'There is always someone worse off than you,' Dad whispered in my ear as we walked towards the check-in desk.

It turned out that Dad had had a stroke that day – a sickening result of clots in his brain. Although it was a relatively small one, it was the first of many that eventually took him away from us.

He had suffered as a child himself. At age 11, he was rushed into hospital after becoming the victim of a schoolboy prank that went terribly wrong. Two young lads who were throwing stones in the street decided to aim one of the pebbles straight at Dad. It went straight into his eye. The surgeons tried their best to save it but they couldn't, so from that day on he had to learn how to live with just the one.

It wasn't easy being a young boy with a glass eye in school. He learnt to live with the jibes, and no matter how self-conscious he felt, he tried not to let it interfere with his dreams. He achieved so much regardless of the disability – he even passed a gruelling heavy goods vehicle driving test later in his life. He wanted the licence so much, mainly because he wanted to prove to himself he could overcome a seemingly impossible obstacle. He also believed it would encourage others suffering from physical differences and disabilities.

Coincidentally, at this point in my thinking, a huge lorry rattled past the taxi, bringing my memories to a halt. I looked up and my surroundings were familiar. I realised that we were in Chesterfield. As the taxi pulled up outside the hospital entrance, I called Paul to let him know I'd arrived. I then sat motionless in the back of the car waiting for him to collect me. My mind churned over the last few hours.

It was during the panic of throwing all my belongings into my case and travel bag when I found out I was too late. My cousin Sandy had called me and she'd tried so hard to keep it from me. She didn't want my journey to be any more difficult than it had to be, but I guessed anyway. I sensed the sadness in her voice.

All the hotel guests must have heard my screams when I realised that Dad had already passed away.

It was a bitterly cold early morning when I finally stepped out of the cab. My watch was barely visible in the dim light of the taxi, but it looked to be around 3.30am. I could see my brother's familiar figure walking towards me.

All I could think about was being with my father. But seeing him lying in the hospital bed only made me feel worse. He was pale, still; there was no sign of his cheeky grin. Reality set in and I realised it hadn't all been a horrific nightmare.

He wasn't going to wake up, and neither was I.

The man I loved so much was now in heaven, but I hadn't been given the chance to say a proper goodbye. Only a few days before, he'd waved me off from their doorstep. That had been our last conversation.

'Are you alright for money, Sharon?' he'd asked me. 'Do you need any help?'

'Dad, I'm fine,' I replied. 'I'm away with work, so they will be looking after me. You be good until I get back home.'

Nodding, he shuffled back into their bungalow. Mum smiled lovingly at her husband, and then turned to me. 'Take care, darling, and keep in touch.' She blew a kiss, waved, and watched me from the doorway until my car was out of sight.

Now here Dad was, lifeless in a hospital bed. I flung my arms around his cold, frail body. He felt colder than the harsh

November air. I ruminated over my last few words to him again and again, and I bawled my heart out.

'Why did you have to go when I wasn't here with you, Dad?' I cried at him through my tears. 'You promised me you'd be good.'

CHAPTER 6

barking mad

A few months after my father's death I managed to convince Mum that we both needed a holiday. Hoping we could go abroad, I coaxed her into applying for her first passport – but I still couldn't quite manage to convince her to fly. Instead we took a more leisurely route, travelling by coach to Dover, crossing to France on a ferry, and then finally taking another coach drive over to Spain.

We stayed in a small seaside resort near Barcelona, and although it was a wonderful little place, we had four days of torrential rain. What a shame that this was Mum's introduction to the Mediterranean. Most of the week's excursions were cancelled, but it didn't dampen our spirits. For the first time since Dad had died, we learnt how to laugh and have some fun again.

But not long after we got back, an all too familiar feeling washed over me. Midway through 2004, depression reared its ugly head once more. I became extremely ill.

Even though I tried so hard to combat it, the sickness dragged me kicking and screaming into the pits of hell. I isolated myself, I didn't want to socialise, and refused to go to work, initially making the excuse that I was suffering from a bad case of flu. The trauma of facing people felt far too overwhelming. I simply wanted to shut the door on the whole world.

Eventually my doctor signed me off sick, stating that I had delayed trauma from my father's death. For almost eight weeks I had barely any contact with anyone other than my mum, brother and best friend Marie. Since Dad's funeral I had been struggling inwardly, trying to stay strong for Mum. My brother was now married and living and working in Liverpool, and although he'd been a tower of strength during the funeral, he couldn't watch over Mum in the way I could.

I must have bottled up so much grief. Considering the downward spiral of my life, it's no wonder I was prescribed antidepressants. Also thrown into the mix was my ongoing battle with low self-esteem, increasing anxiety over my growing debt, and my uncontrollable, compulsive spending. I cried solidly for days, stared up at my living-room ceiling for hours. It certainly wasn't the first time I had been struck down in this way.

But it was my first introduction to Prozac, and after a little while it began to kick in. I started to feel much calmer, as though nothing mattered any more. My brother set up Dad's computer in my living room, hoping it would help occupy my mind and perhaps spark a new interest. It did the trick. I signed up with an internet provider, suddenly feeling drawn into a whole new world. There had been talk at work about the sales team being issued with laptops, but although I had used computers in previous jobs, I also recognised my skills were more than a little rusty. I subscribed to an online dating site, even met up with a couple of the guys. And even though nothing ever happened, it helped to lift my mood. I surfed the internet, intrigued by the endless possibilities.

Feeling almost myself again, I told myself it was time for me to get back into my job. But before that I desperately needed a short holiday and a change of scenery, so I told Mum that I was going away for a few days. I thought maybe a European city break was a good idea, but Mum didn't seem very happy. She didn't like the idea of me holidaying alone, thinking I would be far happier with some company. She wasn't convinced I was fully recovered. The antidepressants had lifted my spirits, but now I was suffering from a nasty skin irritation and it was making me feel miserable.

'Can I go with you?' she asked me with a concerned look on her face.

'Mum, that really limits where I can go. You won't fly!'

It wasn't just flying that scared her. She was also worried about the traumas of being a disabled passenger. Mum had suffered quite a severe stroke in her early fifties, mainly due to exhaustion and stress. Coping with Dad's illnesses while working a full-time job probably triggered it, but through sheer determination she'd almost made a full recovery. Sadly, though, the stroke had damaged a part of the brain controlling her balance. She had learnt to master the handicap at home, but she still needed to use a tri walker when out and about, to keep her independence.

She looked hesitant. 'Okay. Book something, and I will fly just for you. But can we make it a short journey?'

And so, before Mum could change her mind, we booked a trip to Dublin.

Mum squeezed my hand tightly as the plane lifted off for our 40-minute flight. She was incredibly brave, though noticeably relieved when we touched down in Dublin's airport. Her worries about being a hindrance were totally unfounded, since both the airport staff and flight crew were really considerate. For weeks she told her friends about her conversation with the pilot as she waited to be helped off the plane. I honestly believe Mum thought it was part of the hospitality package.

The dismal weather followed us. It was more of an inconvenience to me rather than a disappointment, though. My stress-related skin condition was particularly sore around my eyes and I was forced into wearing sunglasses under the dark clouds and rain. I felt really silly! People kept giving me conspicuous looks as they tried to figure out my reasons for going incognito. It was funny.

The Irish certainly know how to treat their guests, and the Dubliners showered Mum and I with generosity during our visit to their beautiful country. We were welcomed with open arms wherever we went, beckoned into their bars and bought local Guinness to savour.

It was a truly enjoyable weekend, but still I realised that Mum was right about me not being completely healed. I returned to work, but things weren't as they seemed. I was painting a rosy picture of my life and displaying it to other people, but it couldn't have been further from the truth. There was something far more sinister going on inside me, and until I dealt with it, the short periods during which I believed I was "happy" would only ever be temporary. I loathed myself. I hated the way I looked, I hated the way I felt. I was ashamed of my mental health. That self-hate I'd harboured since being a young woman was still there.

I decided I needed something that would help me overcome the trauma of Dad's death.

'Maybe if I organise a charity event it will take my mind off things a little,' I suggested to Mum. It wasn't the first time I'd considered doing a fundraiser.

After my frightening car accident in 1999, I'd decided to give something back to society. If I had learnt one thing from my narrow escape that Friday morning on the M56, it was the realisation of how vulnerable we all are. It's so easy for a story to have a completely different ending than you expected. Lives are changed in a matter of seconds, sometimes through circumstances that can have a devastating effect on the future. And so, although the accident didn't encourage me to make any drastic lifestyle changes, it did encourage me to help others.

Dad had achieved so much for various charities over the years, so I had his expertise to call upon. His illness was already affecting his lifestyle, making it impossible for him to do as much as he would have liked. But I reckoned with my sales and marketing knowledge, coupled with his wisdom and knowledge, we could raise a substantial amount of money. After some words of warning and common-sense tips from my dad, I set about organising my first ever charity event, raising funds for the NSPCC.

I'd asked Glenn Tilbrook, my friend and lead singer from the band Squeeze, to help me out. He agreed to do a solo acoustic gig in between the band's tour dates supporting Blondie, and together on 24th November 1999 we raised a significant amount of money for a worthy cause.

The sense of achievement I got from the event's success far outweighed any euphoria I'd got from reaching work-related targets. And yet oddly enough, I'd never felt compelled to do any more fundraisers until the idea struck me again on the plane back home from Dublin.

The decision to start fundraising again was to help me overcome the pain of losing Dad. And whatever I accomplished would be in his honour.

There was no doubt that he loved helping others. He also enjoyed the stage, which is why he always encouraged Mum to sing publicly. Dad had bags of personality, and he could mix with all types of people, whatever their class or stature. His engaging presence and infectious wit made it incredibly easy for him to captivate an audience, so for several years both my parents worked in the entertainment business. He formed a stage act called Kevin's Kabaret, and they performed in working men's clubs all across England. It acted as a spring board for Mum's semi-professional singing career. The act consisted of Dad – a compere / comedian, Mum – the singer, their magician friend, and his wife who acted as an assistant. The best part is that they also became a fundraising quartet.

I feel fortunate to have been blessed with a lot of Dad's attributes, and I believe that I inherited his desire to help, his confidence in connecting with others, and most of all his resilience when things got tough. I hoped these qualities would help me make the fundraiser a success.

It was late summer in 2004 when I first met Rosemary. She was a long-time volunteer for the NSPCC, and was introduced to me by the charity's appeals manager. She and her husband were keen golfers and members of a prestigious golf club. They were accustomed to taking part in charity golf tournaments.

I sat in the hotel lounge, dressed in my favourite jeans that were deliberately ripped across both knees. They had frayed bottoms that rested upon my winkle-picker red ankle boots. Bleached blonde curls spilled around the sides of my grey cloth cap, which I'd put on to hide my dark roots. A pink fluorescent writing pad lay on the table in front of me. It contained lots of my scribbled ideas, concepts that I hoped would sell my proposal for the charity event.

I don't think Rosemary will mind me saying that, when she first heard my fundraising proposal, she must have thought, *she is barking mad!*

My idea? A celebrity golf day. It must have sounded completely off the wall at first.

Rosemary fired the obvious questions at me after I divulged my thoughts excitedly.

'Can you play golf?' Rosemary asked. 'Do you know any local celebrities who play golf?' She gave me a discerning look.

My answer to both was a resounding no.

I could understand her concerns, especially after my response. But I knew I could do it. I loved a challenge, and I still had a couple of professional footballers' numbers in my phone directory from the 1999 fundraiser. It was a long shot, but it was a start.

It wasn't long before my enthusiasm and passion convinced Rosemary too.

Pulling off this fundraiser wasn't easy. Sometimes it was extremely difficult trying to balance my full-time job as a sales executive with my part-time role as a volunteer for the NSPCC. I would often work into the early hours emailing local sports heroes and celebrities. I sent out countless requests for people to take part in the contest or donate prizes for the raffle. There was no one I considered unapproachable. Rejection didn't faze me.

I got a deep satisfaction from achieving seemingly impossible results. Sometimes the doubters were right, but more often than not I proved them wrong. It gave me such a sense of purpose. It made me phenomenally happy. I almost wanted to give the project my undivided attention, often feeling that my real job was getting in the way.

With some help from Rosemary and some volunteers, over the next two years I turned my wild ideas into reality. On 12th May 2005, we held the first of two very successful celebrity golf days, raising over £8,000.

Rosemary, who had now become a very dear friend, urged me to make the next golf day even more special. 'Why don't we hold the event in your father's name?' she suggested.

"The Kevin Bull Memorial Golf Day 2006" was emblazoned across our flyers and tickets. It headlined our media advertising and was engraved on the winner's cup too.

My dream had finally come true: a fundraiser officially and publicly held in my dad's honour.

On the day I handed over the engraved cup to the winning team, my heart burst with pride. The golf club's lounge area was packed with professional footballers, managers, past sporting heroes, business and media representatives. I turned to face them all and gave my thank-you speech.

'This one's for you, Dad,' I said, looking up at the ceiling. 'I hope I've made you proud.'

There wasn't a dry eye left in the place.

Off the back of our success, I was already being encouraged to plan for a further golf day in 2007, but after the triumph of Dad's memorial competition I decided it was time to take a well-earned rest. I had paid the price for trying to burn the candle at both ends. Exhaustion – combined with my other underlying issues – was putting a strain on my wellbeing.

Even so, I pledged to bring the fundraiser back in 2008, but sadly this never materialised. The company I worked for had diversified into new markets and with increased responsibilities in my working role, there seemed little time for anything else.

It was a strange few years, because although in one area of my life I was obviously ridiculously unhappy – spending a vast amount of money in an attempt to bury my troubled emotions – in another area of my life I was feeling extremely fulfilled, helping to raise a huge amount of money for vulnerable kids. But never did the two intertwine.

I was almost living a dual life. I wasn't quite Jekyll and Hyde, but I definitely had a thorny alter ego, a more dominant player overshadowing my true nature. My need to be seen as a successful, affluent career woman superseded my desire to be of service to others. I listened to my ego far more than I listened to my heart.

In both body and soul, I was far more uplifted when my goal was to make a difference for others. Why couldn't I see this? After a short rest I was twitching to carry on fundraising, and I organised another three events, raising a grand total of £20,000 for disadvantaged children. So why didn't it register that working through my to-do list was never a chore when it was for a charity event? Even during the toughest times, it was an absolute joy. If I was working towards a fundraising target, I focused so much on that that my other issues seemed a lot less important. Why didn't I realise this?

For me, helping others is one of the keys to true happiness. The amazing thing is that I experienced this joy on a few occasions, failing every single time to realise how fulfilled I was during these times in my life.

CHAPTER 7

the butterfly symbol

I have never remembered much about Dad's funeral. There were a few strange things that happened on the day that stick in my mind – for instance, the lady who attended the wake, spoke to everyone, and enjoyed the food. But when I asked who she was, no one knew! I found out later she was a regular gatecrasher at funerals. Apparently, there are people who scan the church notice boards for the times and dates of funeral services so that they can attend. Perhaps it's through loneliness, or the chance of free buffet food. Whichever, it seems like an extremely sad and desperate pastime.

I don't remember any of the readings or my father's eulogy. I only remember Bette Midler's 'Wind Beneath My Wings' playing. She was one of Dad's all-time favourite singers.

One thing that does stick in my mind is the priest's sermon at the crematorium. He was a warm-hearted, caring man, and he seemed so different to the other men of the cloth I knew as a child. Just after Dad passed away he told Mum that the gates of heaven would always be open to her, or anyone else who lived a kind, loving and charitable life. His attitude made sense to me; he considered everyone to be equal – regardless of money, stature, or religion. Mum wasn't a Catholic, but that didn't matter to him.

That was better than when I was growing up and the parish priest would continually pester her to practise Catholicism, telling her it was probably better for our upbringing.

I hadn't been to church for many years, but went back for a short while just after Dad's first minor stroke. I did it because I loved my dad and I knew it would make him happy. Don't get me wrong, I believe in Jesus, maybe more than I ever have. But I have a problem with some of the man-made adaptations of religion, so I prefer to practise my own personal type of faith. I feel that I can learn from my mistakes, try to forgive and be a much kinder person even without going to the one-hour service on a Sunday morning. It's a full-time commitment, one which I am trying my best to maintain. But I feel assured if I ever slip up, I will be allowed to try again and again until I get things right.

My father's face lit up when I walked into 8am mass unexpectedly one Sunday morning. I sat down beside him, and his expression was the picture of happiness. It was so obvious it meant the world to him for his daughter to be with him that day.

"Would you come to confession with me and make your return to the faith complete?" he asked me as we walked out of the church. I nodded in agreement.

The following Saturday I went along with him. I felt extremely nervous but happy to take on board his idea.

It had been an awfully long time since I had knelt in a confessional box saying, 'Bless me Father, for I have sinned.' To be honest, I probably should have written a list, because remembering every transgression over my non-practising years was going to be ridiculously difficult.

But as it turns out, Dad went in before me. As he came out and walked past me, he whispered into my ear. 'Don't worry. I have told the priest all about you. He'll be lenient, so don't worry. You will be fine.'

The whole idea was to be anonymous to the Holy Father, but that had just been blown out of the water by Dad's selfless act for his daughter. This was a priest who listened to my account of years away from the church, yet only wanted to welcome me back with open arms. He didn't want to lecture or judge me. He'd taken Mum under his wing in her time of sorrow.

The same priest read out the unforgettable sermon in the crematorium at Dad's funeral.

'Remember your loved ones are always with you. They may not be seen in body, but their spirit will always remain. Recognise the symbols they send, to let you know of their presence. For example, if you see a butterfly at a poignant moment, be assured this is a sign your passed loved ones are with you.'

Three years after my father's death, a ray of light shone over our family. My gorgeous nephew, Jude Anthony Bull, was born on 2nd May 2006. Most aunties and grandparents believe the children in their family are the best, but without a shadow of a doubt me and Mum believed Jude to be the best.

'You're my favourite nephew,' I've always joked.

His response is always the same. 'I'm your only nephew, Aunty Sharon.'

It was the day of my nephew's christening when what I can only describe as a miracle occurred. The priest's sermon came true.

It was a warm summer's day and there was a delightful atmosphere in the church. Many smiling, happy people joined Jude's mum and dad in welcoming their son into the Catholic faith. I was overjoyed at having been chosen to be a godparent, realising that this responsibility was probably the nearest I would ever get to having my own child.

Halfway through the service, Mum and I watched in amazement as a butterfly floated in through an open doorway near the altar. The priest was just about to pour water on Jude's forehead when it started circling above our heads.

Mum and I turned to each other, obviously both remembering the priest's sermon at Dad's funeral. As the butterfly continued to flutter around all the guests, Mum and I burst into tears of joy. There was only a little sadness. I said under my breath, 'Love you, Dad. I'm so glad you've come to see your grandson on his special day.'

I believe miracles happen every day of our lives, but we don't seem to recognise them unless it's an absolute life changer like winning the lottery. The birth of every living being is a miracle, no matter how small or irrelevant we may think they are.

Dad taught me, on many occasions, the importance of other living creature's lives. Dad saved countless birds and mice from the claws of our cats, then reared them back to full health in the safety of the garage. But it was hard for anyone to believe our family story of the pet goldfish.

We had been watching the pet fish float listlessly on his side in the bowl for quite some time. Realising he was probably dying, my brother and I got quite upset. But Dad wouldn't give up on Goldie that easily. He pulled him out of the water and started blowing gently into his mouth, while tenderly massaging his little wet body. To this day I am not sure if it was a stroke of luck or if Dad did manage to resuscitate Goldie, but it seemed to work. He lived to see a few more months.

Undoubtedly our parents' behaviours shape what we become and how we feel as we get older, so I am certain Dad's kindness towards other living beings rubbed off on me.

Dad is never far away from my thoughts, and although it has taken me a long time to come to terms with his passing, I now relish in the fact that I have a lot of his attributes. I hope I'm now living a life that would make him extremely proud.

CHAPTER 8

trying to buy happiness

On an icy cold January evening in 2005, Marie and I were sitting huddled together in our winter pyjamas on my dark green sofa. We had pulled all the settee's scatter cushions around us while scouring the internet for relatively cheap hotel deals.

'More wine, Marie?' I suggested, moving the laptop off my knee and heading into the kitchen. Opening up our second bottle of shiraz, I shouted, 'London would be perfect, don't you think? We could travel down first class on the train. Our mums would love that!'

I walked back into the lounge with two half-full glasses.

'And we could take them to a show,' I continued. I was already excited at the prospect of using the extra credit limit on one of my Visa cards.

Over the past year I'd been finding things a little more difficult financially. My monthly salary was taking a beating from the repayments on three credit cards, an American Express card, and the mortgage. But for now there was a silver lining and I was itching to start spending again.

We knew that Mum and Margaret (Marie's mum) were both going through an incredibly difficult time. Marie's dad and grandma had passed away a couple of months before Dad did.

Our families had a close bond, especially after our shared tragedies, but coming to terms with the loss of their partners couldn't have been easy. We thought taking them on a short break together would help distract them from their sorrow for a few days.

We enjoyed first-class privileges on the train down to the capital and arrived at St Pancras feeling relaxed. The atmosphere in the station was buzzing, and we were incredibly excited. Stepping down from the train, we chatted eagerly about our plans for the next few days. We giggled while we weaved our way through the hustle and bustle, following Mum's lead as she tactically manoeuvred her tri walker through the crowds.

After settling into the hotel we decided a trip down Oxford Street would be the perfect start to our weekend break. We had already booked to see *The Lion King* that evening and planned to visit Covent Garden on the Sunday.

Shopping was an easy pastime for me. It wasn't long before we were weighed down by lots of high-street carrier bags, overflowing with various brands of clothing, make-up, and perfume. As we drifted in and out of the department stores we started to flag, so we decided to find somewhere to rest our legs. Weary from too much walking and the weight of the bags, we strolled through Soho, searching for a bistro with a menu to whet our appetites.

Our mums were busy chatting to one another a few yards behind me and Marie. Neither had noticed the scruffy looking elderly man heading in their direction. He was dressed in dirty trousers and a raincoat that was probably cream originally but was now miscoloured and covered in deeply ingrained stains. His trouser legs were far too short for him, barely covering his shins. I wondered if they'd been given away to charity after being shrunk in the wash. He wore a pair of frayed burgundy braces over a worn-out shirt. Both looked like they had seen better days, but both were on display because his raincoat no longer had any buttons.

Mum and Margaret were still oblivious to him, but this was all about to change. He stopped next to them and, with a disgusting leer across his face, he cocked his leg as far as it would go and proudly broke wind. He then continued on his way. Margaret and Mum were flabbergasted. The noise travelled across the street, filtering into people's conversations as they sat enjoying drinks outside a pub.

Heads automatically turned towards Mum and Margaret, because by this time the real culprit had disappeared.

Our bellies ached with laughter and we carried on laughing long into the evening. This was just the first of so many fun experiences we would share together. They temporarily blocked out my heartache, sadness, and pain. Hopefully they did the same for Mum, Margaret, and Marie too.

Over the next couple of years I booked lots of holidays, including city breaks and cruises. I spared no expense. I had an inbuilt need for everything to be perfect. After Dad died, my crusade to chase happiness for myself and everyone else became undeniably worse. Bringing joy to others is a wonderful thing – but at this point the only way I knew how to do it was to spend money recklessly. I would secretly book added extras onto our holidays – better cabins, more baggage allowance, and four-star hotels. I lavished myself with fancy dresses, so that on each holiday my suitcase would be bursting at the seams with extravagant items of clothing.

Walking into my favourite boutique in Meadowhall Retail Park always excited me. I was almost like a child in a sweet shop. Within seconds I would scan the shop, and I almost always headed towards the new arrivals rail. My heart would beat louder and louder. My mouth would moisten at the thought of a new outfit to wear. For those 15 minutes – as I pulled back each hanger to look at each individual item – I was deliriously happy.

Their rails were always overflowing with designer names from Versace to Save the Queen, one of my favourite brands. I'd get an almighty buzz when plucking out garments to try on. Members of staff would take them swiftly, eager to help. They'd hang up an assortment of frocks, skirts, and blouses in the stylish changing room and have them waiting for me. They tempted me to try every single one of them individually.

Dressing up in freshly bought clothes was part of my psychological problem. I always felt I stood out from the crowd wearing a brand spanking new outfit. My biggest issue was that once I'd worn the dress, skirt, or blouse it no longer served a purpose.

And there begins the vicious circle of addiction.

While most shoppers would buy their favourite item from a choice of a few pieces, it wasn't unusual for me to walk out of a shop with three or four outfits. Cost was never the first thing on my mind. It should have been, because just like any addiction, the quick fix was very quickly replaced with shame and revulsion. I'd regularly feel anxious and nauseated at my escalating debt. It would only subside for short periods after an increased credit limit, additional loan or credit card.

I was still far away from understanding how to find true happiness. And until I fixed the root cause behind all my squandering, the never-ending splurges were just papering over the cracks, getting me deeper and deeper into debt.

People often ask me why the people closest to me couldn't see that my spending was getting out of control. I have two answers to this. Firstly, at the height of my spending we were all preoccupied with our own personal grief. Secondly, I was an extremely good storyteller – no one would have believed I was racking up so much debt.

It is often said that money alone can't buy happiness, and when I look back over the years at my relentless spending – assuming it would automatically fix my personal issues – I wholeheartedly agree. How often do we use external pleasures as a comfort blanket, hoping to resolve problems that ultimately we can only vanquish ourselves?

Money is a useful resource, and it's one that we cannot live without. It fuels the world we live in today and is necessary for our basic comforts. I hate to say that it's the root of all evil, but through misuse it so often can be.

I also misconstrued happiness with status, believing that the more I had – or was seen to have – the easier I'd be able to find love, admiration, and friendship. I desperately wanted to be respected and needed people to believe in me. I wanted them to see me as a confident and vivacious woman, and yet I didn't even believe it myself.

The notion that we need other people to approve of us is the reason we are so often let down, especially when we hold them responsible for our contentment.

I remember the psychiatrist's words. 'No man will marry you looking like that. Men don't marry women like you!'

I made these words the dogma of my life. Because of this, they have been the cause of many regretful actions, anger, frustrations, and deluded misinterpretations. There is no denying I foolishly cherished my credit cards, seeing them as gifts from heaven when they dropped through the letterbox. I used them to compensate for the emptiness I was feeling within.

The question I needed to ask myself was why I saw shopping as the antidote for my every trauma, dilemma, and predicament, particularly when, after a while, it was no longer making me feel joyful – even for a short time. Those moments of elation, those rushes of adrenaline were beginning to be replaced with a physical sickness at the amount of money I had spent. It wasn't helping that I was making visits to the high street in a working capacity either. It made it all too easy to open my purse. I was trapped in a continual vicious circle of compulsive spending followed by deep regret.

In 2008 I was delivered yet another major warning sign when the financial rug was finally pulled from under my feet.

If you have a small amount of debt, you can pay it off in affordable monthly repayments. This is probably a perfectly acceptable situation to be in, if you're disciplined enough to maintain this level of credit.

Addiction, however – just like any other form of mental illness – can interfere with the normality of life. My debt had become a very serious problem. I couldn't even afford minimum monthly payments on my credit cards.

Life got really tricky, and once I started to miss the minimum repayments, the endless phone calls from my creditors' debt collectors began. They were rarely sympathetic, almost brutal at times. It felt like I was just a number – a statistic, not a human being.

It was the constant threatening phone calls and months of sleepless nights which gave me no other option but to sell my beautiful home, throw away my credit cards, and consolidate my £50,000 of debt.

The spending party was well and truly over.

Insomnia, depression, and anxiety were now part and parcel of my life. And yet I still persisted in closeting the situation. I could put on a good show and keep up the charade, because it was far better than the humiliation of admitting I wasn't perfect. Hiding it was much easier than confessing that I'd failed in society.

I moved into a rented house, but I wasn't truthful about the situation. I preferred to play on the fact that a three-bedroomed house would give me more space for visitors, rather than admit I could no longer afford the mortgage payments.

Ridiculous as this may seem, I was also discussing fostering a child with a government agency, so this gave me another valid reason for needing extra space. I had a genuine desire to be part of a troubled infant's life. I was under no illusions that I was well past the doctor's advised deadline for mothering a child of my own.

The maternal instinct lay heavy on my heart. But as honourable as my intentions were, I have no idea how I thought I could carry the application through with so much debt around my neck. It wasn't until I had passed the police checks and sailed through the first half of my interviews that I finally acknowledged how farcical the situation was and stopped the process going any further with the agency.

Once I had settled into my new home I began to look at the different options available to me for consolidating my debt. Although bankruptcy was one of the alternatives, I thought this would be a coward's way out. I felt I needed to learn some lessons in money management, so I arranged with a financial company to take out their IVA payment plan.

For a little while life regained some normality. Creditors were no longer allowed to call me, and although I was having to live under a very strict budget, I was encouraged at how easily I adapted to a life without credit cards and bank loans. I hoped I could convince my family that nothing was wrong, by telling them I had simply committed to tightening my purse strings. If they knew the true extent of my debt, they would have been horrified.

'That's a wise decision, Sharon,' Mum said. She seemed happy; once again I'd convincingly made light of my situation.

It wasn't rocket science to notice how dire the country's financial state was, or how unstable jobs were becoming.

"UK IN RECESSION AS THE ECONOMY SLIDES."

This was the media's headline news in January 2009. Unemployment was rising at an alarming rate, high-street sales had taken a frightening downturn, and the stress at work became unbearable. The sales team I had worked with for 13 years started to lose their spirit. But after taking extreme measures and selling my home to realign my life, it was about to get a whole lot worse.

It was autumn 2009 and the nights were drawing in. Leaves were falling from the trees and my territory had been extended to cover the North East of England. My journeys were becoming unreasonably long and my working days tiresome. But most of all I was feeling increasingly frustrated with the little time I had left for personal and leisure time. The job had also started to lose its flavour, because over the past 12 months, filling in spreadsheets for the new sales manager had taken precedence over everything else. Due to his never-ending list of admin requests – and to ensure I kept up with his demands – I started working on my laptop for hours in the evening, after a long drive home. I was constantly feeling under pressure. I was highly stressed and agitated, mixing late nights with early morning starts. It was beginning to put a strain on my wellbeing.

One morning, knowing I had a long day ahead of me, I set off for Newcastle Upon Tyne especially early. Having secured a substantial amount of business with a small high-street chain, I wanted to be sure the merchandising was done correctly to encourage sales. So, I planned to visit all four stores and help set up the displays.

It was while I was hoisting my overloaded business bag from the car's back seat that I accidentally slammed my head into one of the steel girders of the multi-storey car park. The pain was excruciating. It seemed to flash from the back of my head through to my forehead. Feeling dizzy – but at the same time worried about getting to my first appointment on time – I simply rubbed the area that had received the blow, locked the car, and headed off to my meeting.

I had a continuous stabbing pain throughout the morning. Even though it was highly likely it was connected to the incident in the car park, I chose to ignore it. A few hours later I was overcome with nausea too, but I simply put it down to exhaustion, being more frustrated by the inconvenience to my schedule. I decided to take an early lunch break, hoping that a bite to eat would help to reduce the constant pounding. But I didn't even manage one spoonful of vegetable soup.

The next two stores I needed to visit were both in retail parks on the outskirts of the city centre. So, determined to continue with my day's work, I bought a packet of painkillers. I hoped they would tackle the dreadful headache enough for me to continue with my day, but after a couple of hours there didn't appear to be any improvement at all.

While I was working on a merchandising stand, my legs began to give way. This was when I realised that there had to be something really wrong. It had to more sinister than just a tension headache. Still very unsteady on my feet – with the pain in my head now almost unbearable – I made my excuses to leave early and set off for what was to be one of my longest and most harrowing journeys home.

I'm not sure how I managed to stay focused behind the wheel of my car. Without every window open to keep me alert, I really doubt I would have made it home. As darkness descended, the lighting from the roadside lamps alongside the A1 motorway conflicted with my vision, putting an extra strain on my driving ability. I battled with the elements for over two hours, as the cold air streamed from the open windows into my Toyota.

To say that I am eternally grateful for arriving home safely that evening is not an understatement.

I didn't want to worry Mum when I got back, and thought that maybe a good night's sleep would cure whatever it was. After taking a couple more painkillers, I hit the sheets. But even though I was feeling completely drained, I hardly shut my eyes.

The severity of the headache never lessened, so the next morning Mum insisted we went to the hospital. She couldn't believe how ill I looked when I called to collect her. Hardly surprising, really, as the hospital doctor diagnosed a severe concussion. He assumed it was triggered by a head injury sustained from my accident in the car park.

As if that wasn't scary enough, he also told me that my decision to drive home the previous evening – and not to go to A&E until the following day – could have had serious consequences. He signed me off sick from work, telling me that under no circumstances should I be driving long distances over the next few days.

Within a week I was back behind the wheel of my car.

I was northward bound. I had almost hit my new business sales target, so I wasn't going to allow anything to get in the way. The potential bonus riding on my success would make so much difference to Christmas. Most of the money needed to go to the IVA, but it would have made present buying a lot easier.

I had no love for the job any more. I had more than proved my professional capabilities, and yet my personal life was almost ruined. Mentally and financially, I was broken.

Once again, I'd heeded another warning sign. And shortly after I went back to work things began to go horribly wrong. The final warning sign was just around the corner, and this time it came complete with alarm bells, red flags and danger signs, so there was no way it could be ignored. Time was running out, because the road I insisted on taking was now becoming perilous for my health. After a gruelling last quarter trying to meet the company's increasing target demands, I came to the conclusion that the only way to salvage what little mental wellbeing I had left was to accept a redundancy package.

I'd been battling anxiety for several months, which was probably triggered by a build-up of work-related stress. I could see where this was heading. Another serious bout of depression didn't seem too far around the corner.

My decision to accept the redundancy wasn't really consistent with the way my role had developed either. During the previous

18 months – even with my health issues, the country's recession, and the new sales manager's aggression – there was still a small element of the job I enjoyed, and that was reaching targets. Through the development of several new accounts, I achieved the company's 2009 targets. But the new boss seemed to have declared war on the sales team. One by one we were being singled out, our passion and hard work decimated by moving goal posts and shady decisions.

Trying to keep up with my increasing job responsibilities was taxing enough, but the manager's head-spinning administrative requests and deadlines were eating into what little personal life I had left. His manipulative behaviour had already scarred some members of the team, and although I tried really hard to keep my head down and ride the storm, my health was being severely affected.

In my last meeting with the heads of the company, they were far from sympathetic about my poor health. But it helped me to make the final decision. I'd been signed off sick for a few weeks with depression and anxiety, but this didn't seem to make any difference to them. It had no effect on where the meeting was held, or how it was done.

Getting ready that morning was hellish. I had a long drive ahead of me to Lancashire. I swallowed my prescribed antidepressant with the last dregs of my morning tea and stared hard at my face in the dressing-table mirror.

'How has it come to this?' I muttered to myself.

It felt as though my whole world was collapsing around me. The idea of losing my job was unthinkable, but it was growing ever more likely. I started to panic, thinking about my debt, my IVA payment plan, and job interviews. I just didn't feel well enough or strong enough for any big life changes.

My breathing suddenly started to quicken. The sound of my heartbeat grew louder and I knew I was about to have a panic attack. This time, though, I acted on the advice of a book I had been reading about meditation. I closed my eyes and began focusing on my breath. I breathed deeply and slowly in and out, calming myself down. Most importantly, it helped to stop the panic attack.

After the meeting – which seemed to drag on for an eternity, but probably lasted a couple of hours – I climbed back into my company car. It was such a relief being back in my own space, though I did wonder how long it would be before the vehicle was taken away from me.

I knew my life was about to change. I felt sick in my stomach at the thought of not having a job, but I hadn't been given much of a choice in the meeting. The only alternatives given to me weren't workable.

The winter weather had taken a nasty turn, making it virtually impossible to drive along Derbyshire's country roads back home. But my battle with the weather was the least of my worries. While struggling with the falling snow, I went through the options the company heads had given me in my head, over and over again. None of them were my idea of a perfect working environment, and so with a heavy heart – knowing I was leaving behind so many great relationships – in March 2010 I left the job I had strived so hard to achieve.

CHAPTER 9

the last few hours

In the run up to February 2010, I'd taken some solace from my distress by organising a charity cabaret event. Once again, the fundraiser was for disadvantaged children. Somehow, amid all the chaos in my life, my wonderful friends and I managed to raise a substantial amount of money. Artists from across the UK descended on one of the oldest theatres in my hometown to perform for the NSPCC. I think this was when I first realised the power of social media, but I never suspected it would play such an important role in a future business.

Even though my redundancy in March dampened my euphoria a bit, the first couple of months afterwards almost felt as though I was on an extended holiday. I'd never been without work and I'd never taken any career breaks, so for a short time it was liberating not to be governed by early morning alarm calls.

It was also during this time that I developed a new love interest. It was smack bang at the height of my turmoil, after we'd connected on social media in 2009. For months I'd been scrolling through artists' profiles on Myspace, trying to create the perfect line-up for the NSPCC cabaret show. I met him on there and we started direct messaging. We'd talk online into the early hours of the morning.

It seemed the perfect situation at the time, meeting someone who was a stranger to the tragedy that was going on in my life. But I did feel like he understood me. I was down on my heels, feeling vulnerable, and desperately in need of someone to show me love. It wasn't a great basis for a true meaningful romance, but the flirtation gave me a few specks of hope.

In early May I decided to spend a few days away relaxing and visiting some workmates who I hadn't seen in over six months. Finally closing the door on months of unsolvable problems had been a weight off my shoulders, so for a little while I was almost back to myself again. I boarded the 11.39am East Midlands train bound for London St Pancras International. Sitting in a very busy carriage on the first leg of my journey, memories of my last business trip to London came flooding back.

'Cheers!' I sipped on a glass of fine champagne in Searcys Bar with another member of the sales team. We were celebrating the success of a long, arduous week at the company's annual exhibition. It was a well-deserved treat for getting through the past five days. We knew the hard work had only just begun. The following few months would be challenging as we tried to sell a targeted number of the following year's ranges to customers.

Now, though, I was alone in a carriage. Travelling alone had never really bothered me. Maybe the nature of my work had helped me to conquer any fears around that. The journey was a great way to relax, and it gave me time to reflect and mull things over in my mind.

I pulled out a piece of scrap paper from my handbag and started to write. I don't know where the words came from, but they flowed with ease from my pen. Reading back the poem to myself, I was startled at how effortless it had been to write. This was my first serious piece of creative writing and –unbeknown to me then – the first seeds of a new journey in my life.

I'd always been a keen scribbler. I'd kept diaries, concocted short silly verses in family and friends' birthday cards. But this was something different.

Not long after returning from my trip, I started to feel bored. The holiday feeling soon descended into despair.

As time went by the days grew incredibly long, the evenings even longer. The hours of lightness and darkness intertwined with each other. It all became a blur, made worse because I was starting to drink more and more. I'd always enjoyed a drink – maybe a little more than I should have done sometimes – but I was a social drinker. My drinking would generally happen at the weekend to celebrate the end of a long, arduous working week. But now my mental state was deteriorating rapidly. Although depression had played an annoying game with me since my late teens, this time the illness was becoming frighteningly worse. Neither the antidepressants, my online love interest, drinking, nor bingeing were making me feel better.

I drank so that I didn't have to think. I shovelled down crisps, chips, pizzas, and chocolate, any type of junk food I could get my hands on. It was all through self-loathing. No one knew what I was doing. Of course, there were the odd tell-tale signs – I started to put on weight – but a pair of leggings and a slouchy jumper seemed to do the trick.

I continued to put pen to paper. Sometimes I wrote verse, other times a paragraph or two of my thoughts. I created a portfolio of poetry and blogs. I toyed with the first draft of a possible book – which later became this one. I got a few Facebook shares when I put the writing online, but at this point I never considered that it could be my free ticket to a much more meaningful life. At first my words were almost always very dark, but sometimes my playful nature would creep up to the surface.

I wrote and scribbled notes until it almost became an obsession. For a few months, I sat until the early hours of the morning thinking up storylines for a still-unfinished novel called *The Return of Mary Cartwright*. It seemed a lot easier to transfer some of my troubles onto the lead character in my book, which I'm sure many authors do.

I was so very messed up. But I realise now that writing was a crucial channel for my emotions during the lowest point in my life.

On 28th April 2011 – just over a year since my redundancy – I was still without a job. I'd been offered a few sales positions, probably due to my good track record with my previous company. There was little doubt I could get results, but on the two occasions I attempted to start a new job, I barely lasted more than a few weeks.

I handed in my notice on both occasions. I still had bad memories from the end of my previous job, and they had a far-reaching effect on me. I just couldn't stand being in that type of working environment any more, no matter how wonderful the company or my colleagues were. My heart was no longer in a career I had fought so hard to achieve for 18 years.

But time was running out, so I needed to find something – and quickly.

My redundancy money pot was almost empty. It had not only been helping me to make ends meet but was also keeping up my IVA payments to keep the creditors at bay. I hadn't felt it was necessary to tell the finance company about my latest predicament, because I was so sure I would find another job before the money ran out. How wrong could I have been?

In between failures, I tested out new waters. I reluctantly signed on at the job centre, along with thousands of others. Nothing seemed to work. I was worrying about the bills and my remaining debt. I felt awful about losing my home. My self-esteem plummeted whenever I had to sign on. Behind closed doors I was becoming seriously ill, already starting to contemplate whether my life was worth living.

*

Shit, here we go! I thought. I screwed up my eyes, hardly daring to peep through the gaps in my fingers. With both feet now firmly on the bathroom scales, I watched in horror. The digits shot from zero, passing eight stone, nine stone, and ten stone, resting on eleven stone three. Where had my perfect figure gone?

The dreaded spare tyre – which, to be fair, was perfectly normal at my age – jiggled and wobbled as I stepped down from the scales. Those scales had told me that I was more than two stone heavier than my ideal weight.

Feeling disgusted with myself, I muttered under my breath, reminding myself of the hard facts. 'You have no life, no job, no man, and no children. Very soon you will have no home. Being two stone overweight is the least of your worries.'

The mirror tells no lies. On this particular spring morning, there was no exception. I stared long and hard at the image looking back at me. My roots were almost two inches long – overgrown as the garden lawns – and my eyes were swollen from a never-ending lack of sleep.

The same question repeated itself over and over again in my mind. *Why me?* I could feel the increasing tension throughout my body. I moved closer to inspect my complexion. My head pounded. I stroked my cheeks and then pulled and stretched the sides of my eyes. I'd always been so proud of my youthful skin, but lines were now starting to appear across my face.

I staggered into the bedroom and flung open the wardrobe door. Although I'd sold or given away a lot of the beautiful dresses that I'd bought during my spending madness, a few were still hanging from the rail. Their sequins, diamantes, and glitter now shimmered in the bedroom light. I ran my fingers across a black taffeta ball gown, purchased especially for a New Year's Eve trip with friends. But then looked down at my size 12 jeans, faded and ripped across the knees. I had always felt my best in a pair of denims, and now they were almost buried under a pile of leggings and baggy T-shirts. I looked back at the handful of remaining designer frocks. They were a sharp reminder of my past addiction, and a reflection of its misconceptions too.

I grabbed a pair of denim-look leggings and an old sweatshirt of Dad's, both of which I had worn the previous day. With hardly anything left to fit me, choosing what to wear was a lot less complicated. Apart from the odd family get-together, there was little cause for dressing up anyway. Positioning myself on the edge of the bed, I pulled on my leggings, looking towards the door as it creaked open. My cat Maddie peered into the bedroom and meowed as she entered, just to make sure I was aware of her arrival. Her great big saucer eyes stared up at me lovingly as she jumped up beside me, rubbing her head affectionately against my arm.

It didn't seem 10 years ago since she had travelled back with me from Liverpool as a six-week-old kitten. She was one of the offspring from a stray cat that my brother's wife had taken in. I instantly fell in love with the little black-and-white ball of fluff. Maddie nudged me again, purring loudly. She snuggled down on my coffee-coloured duvet, appearing to understand that before breakfast I needed to get dressed.

Having pulled on my leggings, I gazed longingly at my late father's sweatshirt. His passing had brought me to my knees, so wearing this gave me some comfort. I missed him terribly, particularly over the past few years. Burying my head into the soft black and grey garment, I bowed my head as tears tumbled down my cheeks.

'He would have known the answers, Maddie, wouldn't he? He would have understood.' Maddie looked up at me sympathetically, watching me weep as she so often did. Once again, I glared at my reflection in the wardrobe mirror. 'What an absolute mess!'

I really was a mess. My mobile credit was almost empty and I knew there wasn't enough money in my bank account to pay all the bills for the following month. And so later that day, I made a reckless decision. I couldn't see any other alternative than to cancel all of my direct debits.

With the laptop perched on my knees and displaying a list of payments and due dates, I hesitated before deleting them one by one. Dripping with sweat, overcome with guilt and feeling nauseated, I nervously logged out of my online banking account.

It was still early afternoon, but the only friend I thought I could lean on – my one and only solace – was an unopened bottle of red wine. Within an hour I was pouring the last droplets into my glass as I cried.

I just couldn't seem to get through a day without crying these days.

I looked around the house as though it was for the last time. I had nothing left of value. I was constantly looking out for anything with even the tiniest potential of raising enough money to help me stay afloat. I'd been selling things on eBay. The first thing to go had been a 1970's original disco mirror. I'd held on to the treasured item for years. I remember my dad returning home with the mirror tucked under his arm years earlier. Hidden under some scrap material, he'd laid it carefully onto the kitchen table.

'What do you think of this, Sharon?' he'd said, pulling the cloth away. He knew I would love it. Some of his old colleagues had been clearing out a closed-down nightclub and automatically thought of me. Dad set about fixing it to my bedroom wall and from then on, everywhere I lived, the mirror came with me. It was always proudly displayed in a hallway, bedroom, or kitchen. I was so disappointed at how much it had raised in the eBay auction. Its sentimental value was immense to me, but I couldn't afford to let sentimentality get in the way. I needed the money to make ends meet.

A Marilyn Monroe picture hung centre stage in the living room. She smiled at me, just as she always did, her lips ruby-red, her flawless face pale, her beautiful hair golden. I barely had anything left of the Hollywood star's memorabilia.

'You'll be the next to go,' I said, tipping the empty wine glass into my mouth, hoping to catch the last few dregs that had settled into the bottom. A huge knot – which for months had lodged itself firmly in the middle of my chest – suddenly started to rise and form a lump in my throat. It was then that my outpouring of sorrow came.

But unlike before, I was inconsolable. I was grief stricken and I couldn't control my tears. I screamed and wailed for the next few hours, feeling completely desolate and utterly heartbroken.

What had gone wrong in my life?

I don't like to be reminded of the times I've contemplated suicide. But – particularly around this time – there were a number of occasions when I considered it. I was always alone, numbed by the effects of drink and antidepressants. Even though I fully understood the devastating impact it would have on my family and friends, I still felt it was the best solution for everyone.

Still sobbing, I grabbed both my Prozac and painkillers. I studied the packaging and contents for a short while, but then I realised I needed more wine to wash them down. So, after throwing the pills on the kitchen table, I grabbed my purse and waterproof coat.

'This one is very nice, and it has a special offer this week.' I could hear the shop assistant's friendly voice in the distance as she pointed towards a bottle of shiraz. I loitered nervously around the collection of red wines. I had walked to one of the local convenience stores close by where I lived. Ashamed of what was possibly turning into yet another addiction, recently I'd been alternating my daily visits between each of them.

'Or perhaps you might like the merlot?' The shop assistant interrupted my thoughts once again. To be perfectly honest, the type of grape in the wine hardly mattered to me any more. But, guided by her choices, I went with the first option. Clutching a carrier bag filled with carb-filled snacks and a couple of bottles of the Australian shiraz, I headed back home.

I breathed a sigh of relief as I stepped inside the house and slammed the door shut behind me. I needed to be certain that no one ever knew my secret, though the only visitor I ever had late into the evenings was the pizza boy delivering my order. I rushed upstairs, changing into the only pyjamas I had left to fit around my ever-increasing waistline. The telephone started to ring as I made my way back down the staircase, Maddie close at my heels. This was Mum's third call of the day and thankfully I was back from the shop in time to receive it.

'How are you? What are you up to?' she asked. I was annoyed by her questions, but it was just because I felt ashamed. As I walked into the kitchen with the receiver against my ear, I lied to her once again.

'I'm feeling so much better today, Mum. Thought I might come and spend the day with you tomorrow.'

It was 6pm according to the silver wall clock. Maddie, eager for her tea, was meowing by my feet. I used her hunger as an excuse and said my goodbyes to Mum.

'I'll call you later, before getting into bed.' Mum's last words rang in my ears as I put the phone on the kitchen table and picked up the pill packets once more.

The following day was a bank holiday, a special one due to Prince William marrying Kate Middleton. No doubt 29th April 2011 would be the happiest day of their lives, but maybe for me it wouldn't occur at all.

Bank holidays barely held any significance with me any more anyway. Every day just seemed the same, no matter what the occasion. Nothing of any importance or consequence ever happened from one hour to the next. As a full-time worker I'd always relished bank holidays, in particular the late August one. Weather permitting, I would usually meet up with friends during the day and we would enjoy drinks in the late summer sunshine.

This all seemed in the distant past though. Usually a social butterfly, my self-confidence was dropping at a rate of knots. I couldn't seem to handle people in the way I used to – I was always misjudging and sceptical of their motives. Yes, my dignity had been bruised from the redundancy, but I also think I was unknowingly carrying around an awful lot of bitterness and anger.

I curled up on the huge brown sofa, stuffing my face with a family-sized bag of crisps. It was a tiny grasp at comfort for a woman totally on the brink. In almost seconds I drained a full glass of wine.

It was like something from a Bridget Jones movie, only far more tragic. I guess waking up in the small hours of the morning still clutching an empty wine glass – as I'd done before – was more in line with an AA advertisement. The times I'd woken from an alcohol-induced sleep, startled awake by either the telephone or Maddie's gentle tapping against my leg!

Sometimes Mum, feeling frantic, had rung me to find out if there was a problem because she'd kept calling me without any answer. Sometimes I'd see Maddie's big eyes staring up at me, wondering why I had missed bedtime. Sometimes if I managed to stagger up the stairs, I would find her curled up on my side of the bed, snoring softly.

I poured my second glass of wine and looked over at the pill packets lying by my side. If I was going to take my own life, I needed to drink so that it would hopefully numb my final moments. I thought about the royal wedding the next day. The country would be in full celebration mode, feeling jubilant and happy. But did I really care? I wanted so badly to find some sort of peace, a way out of the turmoil. And solutions seemed very thin on the ground.

The only answer for me – the only sure way to put an end to the ongoing anguish – was to commit suicide.

There have been a few times in my life where all things felt horribly unimaginable. My present circumstance ranked high above any of these. I hated that Mum was becoming more aware of my suffering. I picked up the pill packets and clutched them tightly to my chest. I knew I either needed to end this quickly or tell her the truth. Mum's heart was breaking and I was on the brink of losing my home.

It was time to accept defeat, whichever way I chose to do it.

CHAPTER 10

single bed

I didn't take my life that night.

Fortunately, the alcohol got the better of me and I fell into a deep sleep. I woke up in the early hours of the morning, sitting upright on the sofa with my head almost buried in my chest. I was still clutching the pill packets tightly in my hand.

My body swayed from side to side as I staggered clumsily to my feet, kicking over a wine glass. The shiraz spilled across the wooden floor, and I stared for a few seconds, watching it creep towards the living-room carpet. Feeling disgusted with myself, I picked up the empty glass and stumbled into the kitchen. Placing both the glass and the tablets onto the dining table, I glanced over at the clock. It read 4.30am.

My suicide plot had failed. Maybe the urge to take my own life was never strong enough.

I'm sure there's always been a quiet, gentle voice of reason inside my head, telling me I'm much stronger than this. But for some reason I seemed to delight in listening to the less comforting, harsher voices in my head. They yelled at me, telling me that there was nothing I could do, my situation would never change, and that no one was interested in my predicament anyway. Drinking to excess helped my conscience block out the fact that I was lying to everyone around me, telling them that nothing was going wrong.

It was tough enough to acknowledge how reliant I had become on alcohol, but it was even more distressing for me to accept the reasons why I constantly felt the need to be intoxicated.

Remembering the spilled wine, I walked unsteadily over to the cleaning cupboard and pulled out a cloth to wipe the floor. The shiraz seemed to have just stopped short of the brown-and-cream carpet, which was quite a relief. After mopping it up, I threw the soiled cloth into the kitchen sink and clambered up the stairs to bed.

It hardly seemed worth laying my head on the pillow with less than an hour to go before sunrise. I could hear the birds singing and the dawn light was already starting to creep through a crack in the bedroom curtains.

But if I was finally going to face Mum later that day, I needed a clear head.

Maddie was fast asleep on the bed. She was curled up with her head resting on the far-side pillow. She didn't take too kindly to the disturbance, and I struggled to get the duvet from underneath her. She looked up at me in disgust as I climbed into the bed by her side. I have grown up surrounded by family pets, and in particular cats. It is true what they say about them, though – they do tend to think what's yours is theirs. Maddie believed she had rights to every corner of the house, all three bedrooms and, if she could beat me to it, my side of the bed. She was spoilt and adored, so she nearly always got away with it too.

It was almost ten o'clock when a distant, shrill ringing disturbed my sleep, and I clambered for my phone. Having probably tried to wake me after I crept in beside her, with a few gentle taps on my forehead, Maddie had gone downstairs in a sulk.

Mum was on the other end of the line, asking if I was coming to see her. She seemed quite concerned that I was still in bed, but somehow, I managed to convince her I had been writing long into the early hours of the morning. More deceit, more fabricated stories to cover up my self-destructive lifestyle, a way of living that could only end in disaster. Cringing, I put down the receiver after telling Mum that I'd be with her in the next couple of hours.

The butterflies were already starting to gather in my stomach, because I knew it was time to come clean. I couldn't carry on like this. I had lost everything; I had no energy and had no future means for income. I was fast running out of options. There seemed to be nothing worthwhile to cling on to any more as I realised that all my hopes and dreams had been wiped from under my feet.

I'd lost my social standing; it had been stripped away from me through my own sheer stupidity. But did all the blame just lie with me? What about the banks? What about the financial system, which had encouraged me to pump up my loans and max out my credit cards? Why hadn't they asked more questions about my ability to repay? Or, for that matter, the state of my mental health?

Sometimes all it had taken was one short phone call, and within an hour my credit limit was increased.

Telling Mum about my financial predicament was one of the hardest decisions I ever had to make. I sat down with her and told her about my finances, the years of deceit to cover my tracks, and my suicide attempt. It was incredibly difficult. I'm not sure where I even began, but I watched the tears roll from her cheeks as I desperately tried to fight back my own. When I finally stopped talking, she beckoned me over to her and flung her arms around me.

'This is grim, Sharon. But we will deal with this together now,' she said, sobbing. 'You are no longer on your own.'

My tears fell onto her shoulder. I hadn't felt such relief and comfort for so long.

During the delicate conversation, Mum also shared with me a surprising revelation about her and Dad. My parents had suffered a bankruptcy too.

They'd kept it a secret for years, but it made sense now as to why she'd been so compassionate and sympathetic about what I was going through.

Hearing about Dad's bankruptcy was devastating. Apparently, it had happened a few months after Paul was born. Dad had worked as a painter and decorator since school, so after achieving his City and Guilds he decided to set up his own company. Due to a number of outstanding payments and theft from some of his workforce, the business sadly collapsed, leaving my parents riddled with debt. The consequences for both of them were horrendous.

There may have been some naivety on Dad's part; he was young and wanted to make his way in life. But just like any entrepreneur with a family to look after, his heart was in the right place.

My parents need not have gone through what they did. Surely my father could have been helped by financial advisors, guided through his company's money issues. But instead all he and Mum could look forward to was fear, heartache, and humiliation. Mum told me that she would hide under the table when bailiffs knocked on the door, to take away any saleable household goods to pay off some of their outstanding debts. She was, cruelly, then given the first option to buy back some of their unsold furniture.

'They couldn't charge me a lot,' Mum said. 'We hadn't got the money.'

Understandably it was hard for her, but she relived every dreadful moment so that she could console me.

I have no doubt that the stress of the bankruptcy is what triggered the numerous illnesses which plagued my dad's life.

After hearing Mum's heartbreaking confession, I became even more convinced that society is never very keen to help us during times of failure. It will always be quick to make us feel inadequate, if we allow it to.

This made me think back to my own experiences, when I had to endure cold-hearted and callous telephone calls from the bank's debt-collecting agencies. Without fully understanding my situation, a few of their staff seemed to delight in my misery. Their voices were harsh, and they made me feel inferior. Sometimes it felt as though they wanted to kick me while I was down. They'd answer in a cruel and cutting manner whenever I explained that I had no money to pay off the debt.

I could definitely relate to what my parents went through, but the animosity must have been so much greater all those years ago. Uncomfortable encounters leave their mark on unsuspecting victims, which is why we tend to be so much more critical of ourselves when things go wrong.

Mum understood that I wanted to keep my independence, so initially she tried to help me by subsidising my bills and rent payments. But this was never going to work on a permanent basis without me having some form of income. I was not in a good way mentally, and with no idea what I wanted to do with the rest of my life, finding and maintaining a job was proving extremely difficult.

I continued to write, publishing my verse on social media under the name Pisces Lady. I even sold some bespoke poetry for weddings and christenings. I found these the most laborious to write, but I think that's because it didn't come from the heart. I needed to earn a living though, so the small amounts I made from this type of verse contributed a little towards the household bills.

I eventually set up my own website, but it didn't change the negative outcome from my countless submissions to agents, publishers, and magazines. I received hundreds of rejections, and yet family and friends seemed to love my work. But it wasn't just family and friends I needed to impress. If I was to be taken seriously by anyone in the literary world, then my work had to reach a much wider audience, and I had to jump over this hurdle. Having also registered the reality that poetry alone wasn't going to get my name on the high street's bookshelves, I decided to submit the first three chapters of my novel *The Return of Mary Cartwright*. Once again, though, I received nothing but polite refusals in return.

I started to draw a blank as to where my creativity was heading, if it was going anywhere at all. Nonetheless, I carried on writing. It was as if I knew that one day everything I had gone through – all the knock backs, brick walls and rejections – would eventually make sense.

Creativity was also important to my healing process. During the darkest hours, my laptop became a release mechanism. At first it was a cry for help, but then it became a therapeutic exercise, an aid to my recovery. To quote Gustave Flaubert, "The art of writing is the art of discovering what you believe."

My turbulent emotions spilled onto the page as my fingers typed vigorously. Paragraphs knitted together miraculously, verse flowed with ease, each line triggered from the heart.

In the meantime, I was starting to believe I had a future. Knowing I was no longer facing my debt situation alone – while also discovering my creative talent – I was slowly getting stronger.

Sadly, my finances weren't getting any stronger. I still didn't have a regular employment or a real source of income. I'd eaten into most of my redundancy payment way before telling Mum about the serious predicament I was in. The money had given me some time, helping me to put off the inevitable. I'd used the biggest share of it to keep up with my rent, bills, and IVA payments, but there was no way Mum could continue subsidising my cost of living.

So, towards the end of 2011, I put the small amount of furniture I had left into storage, packed my bags, and reluctantly waved goodbye to my independence. I moved back in with Mum. I had no choice – it was the only thing I could do.

I had now been given the opportunity to rebuild, to start from scratch. Okay, so I hadn't found the love of my life, I didn't have children, I hadn't got a job, and I was also up to my eyes in debt. But moving in with Mum was a life-saving decision.

The past couple of years had been clouded by bad habits, mainly heavy drinking and food bingeing, both quick fixes to block out my true feelings and the issues I needed to face. My mental illness was real, and it was nothing to be ashamed of, but I needed to inject some positivity into my life. I needed to do this so that I could control my depression and anxiety more responsibly.

My shopping addiction had also left a huge void, one that needed to be filled. I wanted to try to replace the antidepressants – which had been prescribed for me on and off for several years – with more natural methods of stabilising my emotions, such as meditation and mindfulness. I had read so much about these practices in library books. I was appreciative of the Prozac and its effectiveness on my severe mood swings. But now I wanted to try incorporating some healthy habits into my daily routine, so that eventually I was no longer reliant on the drug.

I had been given a second chance, another crack at life. I needed to gain strength from my experiences, instead of wallowing in self-pity. It was time for reflection, a time for me to try to understand the root cause behind the shopping addiction, the countless bouts of depression, and my continual low self-esteem.

If I was going to lift myself from the hellish nightmare I'd been through, I needed to remind myself of the positives of those 30 years since I'd left school. I needed to remind myself of the times when my sheer determination – even when I didn't have qualifications or much ambition – helped me fulfil a dream.

I do know that I was almost certainly motivated and driven for the wrong reasons. Much of it was because of my lack of self-worth. But I'd proved that if I was interested enough to achieve a goal or take on a challenge, nothing would hold me back. I was good at reading, studying, and practising, soaking up information like a sponge. Surely I could invest this level of passion into creating a more authentic lifestyle for myself?

With a doting mother taking me under her wing, I knew I was extremely lucky. Without her help I might have been dead, or at least homeless. Mum even offered to let me have her double bedroom while she took the visitor's box bedroom, but I was adamant she had already done more than enough.

So, it was back to a single-bed occupancy for me.

Before Christmas I had finally contacted the IVA company, explaining that I was no longer able to continue with my payments. The agent was extremely considerate about my change of circumstances, and over the next few months they arranged meetings with my creditors to see if they would accept what I had already paid as a final payment. All but one agreed to write off the rest of my debt, which infuriatingly turned it into a failed IVA plan, cancelling out everything I had already paid. I would once again be vulnerable to my creditors if I didn't seek help, so once the festivities were over Mum came with me to the Citizens Advice to find out what could be done.

A small payment plan was put in place, and I started to rebuild my life.

We celebrated the new year in her small two-bedroomed bungalow, vowing that 2012 would be a turning point. We would face our issues together.

CHAPTER 11

exchange of apples

I needed to replace some of my bad habits with good habits. There would be no more quick, temporary fixes to resolve negative emotions or disappointments.

I kept fit through exercise and walking. I spent a lot of time around nature, a delightful reminder of my childhood years and my love of the countryside. Meditation, mindfulness, and writing all helped me to filter out my desire to spend, overeat, or drink too much.

Over the new year I'd been completely engrossed in book called *Instructions for Happiness and Success* by Susie Pearl. It seemed to explain true happiness perfectly. At the same time, I was also reading and digesting articles about humanity's misconception and obsession with success. I could see where I had been going horribly wrong.

I found out that the writer ran various workshops, and one that instantly struck a chord with me was her meditation course. I was already trying to master the concept, but I wasn't overly confident that I was doing it correctly. So, thinking that maybe I needed some expert guidance, I decided to book myself on to the Sunday morning workshop. Mum kindly offered to pay for it – she'd heard me rave about the positive results it can have in changing years of negative thinking. She knew I was really intrigued by the practice and thought it could help with my recovery.

I knew that a complete lifestyle makeover would take some trial and error, but I was also trying to wean myself off the antidepressants. I confined my drinking to nights out or family get-togethers. But it was during a night out with friends – after months shunning social events – that I discovered my partying days were well and truly over.

It had been a wonderful evening; we visited wine bars and bistros in one of Sheffield's more fashionable areas. But I found it difficult to keep up with the pace, and later I embarrassingly fell asleep in a nightclub while my friends danced into the early hours.

It was then that I realised my likes, dislikes, and pastimes were starting to change dramatically. My metamorphosis had begun; I was transforming from the person I'd long grown accustomed to into someone else. I was a total stranger even to myself.

I took the meditation class on a beautiful spring Sunday morning in May 2012. I made my way to Chelsea from South Kensington Station. Although it was a fair walking distance from the venue, I knew I had plenty of time, so I wanted to capitalise on the warm sunshine and the auspicious sights of London town. Halfway there I decided to stop off at a charming little bistro for a drink. Enjoying the sunshine on my face, I lazily watched the fresh lemon slices and ice cubes gently bobbing around in my glass. I had been served by the cutest waiter, who'd showered me with compliments, making my day even more perfect.

I took a sip from the ice-cold drink, my mind wandering down memory lane. I remembered my first holiday abroad with friends, away from the watchful eye of our parents. We were almost giddy with delight because the local boys had been charming us. We were fresh-faced 18-year-olds, enticed by their romantic gestures. Needless to say, my first holiday romance with a somewhat dubious Spanish waiter wasn't all that momentous. As it turned out, I did pick up a few educational tips, learning the hard way that some young men are not to be trusted.

Something seemed very special about that day in 2012. I felt a sense of calmness and tranquillity. Even the long wait for my change and receipt didn't alter my mood. The waiter finally returned, full of apologies. 'So sorry, Madam, for your wait. I was trying very hard to lengthen your visit with us,' he suggested cheekily.

It wasn't long before the class now, and my excitement began to take hold. Somehow, I knew this was going to be the most amazing experience for me. I felt sure that after this introductory course I would adopt the practice of meditation. I wanted it to become a part of my daily routine, to benefit my health. I no longer wanted my destructive habits to endanger it. I had registered that I was changing as a person, already realising that many things that once seemed ultra-important no longer impressed me.

A perfect example of this was my unusually brisk walk through Harrods the previous day. It had been impossible for me to catch a train early enough on the Sunday morning to make the workshop on time, so after settling into my hotel room I decided to make the most of a late Saturday afternoon. Choosing to take a leisurely stroll into Knightsbridge, I stalled as I approached the store's grand entrance. For old time's sake, I nervously passed by the shop's welcoming doorman and stepped into the stylish accessories department.

I soon realised that the excitable adrenaline rush that used to wash over me had been replaced by a nonchalant, laid-back attitude. The smell of expensive perfume and the sight of designer handbags – perfectly displayed alongside fancy evening gloves and diamante necklaces – barely caused me to raise my eyebrows.

It had been extremely tough to overcome the powerful, impulsive urges which had me constantly reaching for my credit cards, but the fact that I was no longer influenced by the glamour, alluring atmosphere, or assistants dressed from head to toe in the latest fashion trends was such a relief.

None of this had anything to do with my inability to spend on plastic. Nor was it because I was frustrated by my financial constraints. It's just that my desire to buy these luxuries had simply vanished.

The past few months of replacing bad habits with good ones, enjoying new interests and reigniting childhood passions were starting to pay off. For almost four years I had been unable to reach for a credit card at a whim. My lifestyle changes – and possibly the haunting memories of what I had gone through with my addiction – had given me the inner strength to resist the store's seductive merchandising. I couldn't be tempted to look through the luxury products, let alone buy any of them.

This was just one aspect of my life that was turning itself on its head. I often had to pinch myself to check I was still Sharon Bull.

A small group gathered together for the meditation workshop. The hotel room was delightful, with large windows looking out onto a patio area. A jug of water and glasses were placed on a table by the door, and plants and candles were dotted around on dark wooden furniture. Chairs had been set out and were facing the windows. There was a serenity about the place before we even started the class.

The combined energy in group meditation is unbelievably powerful. It brings about a positive atmosphere and a unified calmness. Susie's step-by-step guide, Transcendental Meditation, was easy to follow. It's a form of meditation which can be practised anywhere, by anyone. Together we learnt breathing techniques, enhanced our awareness skills and mastered a few short mindfulness sessions. We closed the class with a final lengthier meditation.

Everyone in that room wanted to feel the benefits of being able to sit for a short period of time and calm their mind. That's easier said than done for a lot of people, particularly for those with a mind like mine. I realised, though, that one simple way of getting some reprieve from my constant ruminating and criticising past events in my life was to meditate daily. I felt so elated walking out of the hotel.

After the meditation workshop, I walked back casually towards South Kensington Tube station, chatting about the experience with one of the workshop attendees. We bid our goodbyes at the entrance of the underground and he disappeared into the bustling crowd. I carried on walking back to the hotel. I felt wonderfully strange. It's a hard feeling to explain.

I sauntered along the streets of London, soaking up the mid-afternoon sunshine. I had a flower in my hand and a fresh, juicy green apple tucked safely in my small cloth handbag. Both had been offered to me as gifts at the meditation class to symbolise abundance and happiness.

I had planned to stay another evening, having arranged to meet my online date for tea. I couldn't have possibly called it a romance, although he generally told me what I wanted to hear. I suppose that it been comforting for my bruised and battered ego for quite some time.

I glanced at my mobile to check whether he had texted me back. There was nothing, but that wasn't unusual.

Nor was the sight of a homeless person huddled in a doorway.

Since losing my house I'd been brutally aware of how easy it can be to end up on the streets. I was fortunate that family had taken me in, but without this I could quite easily have been another statistic, one of the increasing numbers of homeless people across the UK. Having recently been volunteering at a shelter, my eyes had been opened to the many scenarios that can force someone from the safety and comfort of their home, including being ex-military, divorced, bankrupt, or a victim of house repossession. Unaffordable rent increases, redundancy, debt, mental health issues, addiction and abuse can also lead to people sleeping rough in alleys and shop doorways, visiting food banks, or begging on a street corner.

As I walked past the homeless lady – who looked to be middle-aged – her desperate plight touched my soul. Her eyes met with mine, stopping me in my tracks. I instantly wanted to reach out to her. With tears in my eyes, I turned to approach the crouched figure, saddened by how little she had. She clung tightly onto what seemed to be her only possession – a tired looking rucksack that probably doubled up as a pillow.

'Would you like an apple?' I asked. I pulled the fresh, juicy piece of fruit from my bag and handed it to her.

I have never seen such gratitude in someone's eyes. She thanked me before eagerly tucking in to the fruit. I walked away, tears streaming down my cheeks.

Once back in my room, I couldn't get the homeless lady out of my mind. I had an idea, but first I needed to pop my flower into a glass of water. I checked my mobile phone again for messages, then headed back out towards a supermarket close by the hotel. I moved swiftly up and down the aisles, filling up a basket with food and drink. I got sandwiches, crisps, water, orange juice, cake, and fruit – the lady in the doorway deserved to have a teatime meal just as much as I did.

Thankfully, she was still there when I went back to her with the two carrier bags of goodies. I don't think she could quite believe her eyes. It was heartwarming to leave her smiling, enthusiastically unpeeling one of the sandwich wrappers.

Back at the hotel, it came as no surprise when I finally received a message from my date. He made excuses as to why he couldn't make it for tea, but I wasn't going to let the disappointment ruin what had so far been a beautiful day. Besides, I was in an unusually relaxed frame of mind, brought on through a combination of walking, sunshine, and meditation. After eating a meal complemented by a delicious glass of red wine, I was more than ready to hit the sheets.

The following morning, I meditated alone for the first time. I was in my hotel room, on the 27th floor. I set my mobile timer for 20 minutes and then, after looking out at the most awesome view of the capital city, I closed my eyes.

To clear my mind of wandering thoughts, I chanted the personal mantra that Susie had given me at the workshop. It opened a floodgate, and my emotions spilled out – emotions that were normally locked, bolted, and screwed down inside my mind. Eventually a calmness and sense of tranquillity washed over every inch of my being.

It was a strange experience, but I sensed that if I incorporated the practice into my daily life, eventually it would help me to analyse the past, present, and future much more clearly and easily. It would help me make my life a far more fulfilling experience moving forward.

Since the first time I tried meditation, I've composed a few mantras of my own. I use them not only in meditation, but when I'm walking and training too. They are positive statements that cut out the mind chatter. Repeated often enough, they can help create a more positive state of mind.

They can be simple statements, such as "I can, I will!" and "Compassion be my guide, compassion by my side, compassion all around me, compassion in my heart."

Packed and ready for my journey home, I glanced around the hotel room one more time to check whether I had left anything behind. The gorgeous flower I had received at the workshop was blossoming in the glass of water, so I didn't have the heart to stunt its growth by packing it into my case. Instead I left it on the dressing table, with a note for the cleaner. *Please look after this flower*, it read. *Enjoy its beauty!*

I didn't take either of the gifts I'd been given on the course home with me – neither the fresh green apple nor the flower.

I stood by the lift, waiting to be taken from the dizzying heights of the hotel's top floor down to their ground floor reception. In my white denim jacket and cut-off jeans, I looked over at the black-and-white Mary Quant style luggage by my side. These were the final remnants of my past. I smiled, thinking about how contrast had been so important to me, down to the last minor detail. Even my suitcases had needed to compliment the outfit I was wearing.

Busy in my thoughts, I almost missed one of the hotel staff as he breezed past me, cheerily bidding me good morning.

But what happened next was very strange. He suddenly stopped in his tracks, turned back around and came towards me, holding a huge bowl in his hands. It was brimming with fresh, juicy green apples.

'Would you like an apple, Madam?' he asked me. I could barely hear his words.

With my mouth still wide open in shock, I gratefully plucked an apple from the top of the pile. I thanked the young man and popped it safely into my handbag, still trying hard to convince myself that the incident had just happened.

Could this have been "the law of attraction" which I had read so much about – the concept of like attracts like? Do we receive back into our lives what we give out, such as negative thoughts, generosity, greed, or kindness? There was no doubt that I'd been consumed with compassion for the homeless lady in the doorway, but it was a little bit scary to think that the hotel worker had almost mirrored my actions.

Maybe it was just a twist of fate, a coincidence. A coincidence that had me waiting for a lift on the 27th floor of the hotel at the exact moment a member of staff walked by with a bowl of green apples. Not a bowl of bananas, or even red apples – but a bowl of fresh, juicy green apples.

I was still debating this in my own mind when the lift's voice announcer cut into my thoughts. 'Ground floor!'

Neither a sceptic nor a believer of the law of attraction, I vowed to keep an open mind and educate myself more.

We choose what we want to believe. Nothing has any power over our minds unless we decide to let irrational thoughts take control. I had allowed this to happen far too often, always presuming the worst-case scenario, regularly jumping to the wrong conclusions. I always assumed that I had no value, believed that my point of view was of little consequence.

This was where I hoped the meditation would help me gain some strength. But, after several months of religiously bringing the discipline into my daily activity, I was extremely worried. I became more frustrated more often. My self-loathing peaked, rather than diminished. My angry outbursts got far worse. My late-evening conversations with my online date turned futile. I grew suspicious, wondering whether he was married. Our nice chats erupted into heated arguments.

I just couldn't understand why this was happening, and so I devoured more library books on the subject and called Susie Pearl to ask for her advice. Through this, two important issues came to light.

Firstly, it turned out that meditation was making me much more aware of my thoughts and feelings. I was becoming an observer of myself, which explained why I was more conscious of my frustrations, self-loathing, and anger.

Secondly, Susie explained through metaphor, my mind was like a small pond that had been left dormant for many years. The mud, silt, sludge, and garbage which had settled deep down at the bottom of the water were like my past issues that I had never dealt with. The meditation process was a big wooden stick stirring the pond, shifting everything from its base and bringing it to the surface.

In other words, my years of mindless thinking, hidden fears, and buried grievances were now all staring me in the face. And now I could deal with them head on.

I weathered the storm as Susie suggested to me, holding on to the theory that sometimes things have to get worse before they get better.

The romance never fully blossomed between me and my online date, but then when relationships are not meant to be, the best option is to walk away. I hadn't closed the door soon enough, and the situation had interfered with my early stages of meditation. I'd allowed anger to creep in and take the leading role.

Meditation became a huge part of my life and changed my outlook massively.

To find out more about Transcendental Meditation, or find a certified teacher in your area, please visit **www.tm.org**

CHAPTER 12

turning point

Mum and I started to rebuild my life together.

The past few years had taught me so much, but a couple of key issues still needed to be addressed properly if I was going to finally turn the corner. Throughout my career – no matter what I'd achieved or how far up the ladder I'd climbed – I'd never once felt the same sense of purpose as when I was organising and planning my charity events.

Surely my passionate commitment to worthy causes should have been an indication of where my heart and soul were best suited. But just like many careerists, my working life was spent mindlessly in the fast lane, so it would never have dawned on me to consider a change in direction.

I had also found in recent months that being creative gave me a new kind of energy, a stimulation which was not only good for my mind, but my wellbeing too. This couldn't have been a clearer message: I needed to use my writing talents to make my way in the world. My blogs and verse had taken up a new format, sending out messages of hope to others while also raising awareness about issues close to my heart. There had to be a way of turning what I loved into a living.

But without much of an idea of how to channel all this new-found knowledge, I still needed to earn some money.

I tried Party Plan, a scheme in which I sold skincare cosmetics, costume jewellery, and handbags. I signed up with temping agencies and applied for countless jobs. Nothing seemed to work. The only solution to me, the only choice that seemed to make perfect sense, was to somehow forge a career as a writer / blogger. My thoughts also turned to public speaking, and I wondered whether this was another window of opportunity for raising awareness and sharing my own experiences.

I knew self-employment wasn't easy though. Up until the end of 2010 I'd been involved in organising a few events at a mate's bar. It had helped me to mingle and meet new friends, and so I'd hoped it could be a springboard to a different career. I'd chosen to start a party-planning business called Monroe Events, but it hadn't worked out. One of the last events I'd been involved with was a Christmas ball, and I hadn't even attended it. Instead I'd sat at home drinking wine and feeling sorry for myself, disgracefully leaving my mum and Marie to stand in my place. The business folded almost as soon as it had started, an example of how easy it can be to quit at the first hurdle.

It was a small taster of how hellish it is to survive.

I had had to claim Jobseeker's Allowance on several occasions. I hated receiving government handouts; it wasn't something I could ever get used to. Whenever I walked into the building to sign on I felt degraded, humiliated about my unemployment. And yet, there were so many other people just like me. There were people of all age groups there, people of both sexes and from different nationalities. Maybe some of them felt the same sense of shame that I did.

Most of the staff were reasonably considerate of this, but there always had to be one bad apple. Unfortunately for me, she conducted my first appointment of 2013.

For the first time I hadn't completed my job hunting objectives. It was Christmas time and I'd spent most of the holidays with family. But this didn't register as an excuse with this member of staff and she declined my next payment.

It was almost as if she enjoyed it. It was like she was depriving a naughty schoolchild of a week's pocket money as a deterrent for future misbehaviour. I was mortified by her smug, cold attitude, but couldn't help thinking how intimidating she would have seemed to an inexperienced youngster.

This horrid experience gave me another kick in the direction towards self-employment, so after writing a letter of complaint to the job centre, I stopped the jobseeker payments and ventured into what was completely unknown territory to me.

It wasn't long before I was surfing the internet to find out more information about public speaking, borrowing "how to" books from the library and contacting speaker agencies. I had added another string to my bow, an occupation that could work alongside my writing.

Stepping entirely out of my comfort zone, I half-blagged my way into the motivational speaking circuit. It was a reminder of how I acquired my first sales position. After being asked in my interview if I was a competent motorway driver, I'd said a very convincing "yes", even though I'd never done it before. I got the job, and so with only a month before my start date, I knew I had my work cut out to gain as much experience on the motorway as I could. So, with my dad by my side for support, I repeatedly drove along the various motorways within my sales territory.

It's surprising how much we can achieve if we tell ourselves we can do it – and then put in the hard work.

Over the next few months I attended some networking meetings. I soon realised that there were quite a few local motivational speakers and coaches doing the circuit, so I tried to see as many of them as I possibly could. Some held their own workshops, while others held talks at various Mind-Body-Spirit festivals. I also managed to book myself on to a couple of events as a speaker, even though I had very little experience or any idea how I was going to deliver my presentation. I knew I had so much to offer others with my story, but the speech needed to be different. The talk had to draw people into my world, for them to get maximum benefit from my experiences with mental health issues, addiction, debt, and recovery.

I also organised a couple of events, which was relatively easy because I had the background knowledge from the charity events I'd run in the past.

It was the summer of 2013 when – through my involvement with a community radio station – I met Paul. Paul was not only one of the station's directors, but he was also a mentor for new business start-ups. Once again, I fearlessly stepped outside the box when I offered to produce and host a couple of two-hour radio shows. With limited knowledge, I overcame the fear of the studio's technology, getting as much information and advice as I could from a few of the established broadcasters.

I invited guests to the show, played the music I liked, made a few faux pas and felt extremely proud that I had managed to pull it off. At the time I probably saw myself as the next Jo Whiley or Vanessa Feltz. While that didn't happen, I believe that it happened for a reason, and it paved the way to the next step in my career.

I had so many visions of what my business would look like, but I wasn't sure how viable they all were. Nevertheless, I approached Paul and asked if I could see him, half expecting to come away from the appointment disappointed. I went to him armed with a portfolio containing samples of my written work, business goals, and ideas.

I was proved wrong. He was incredibly supportive, and believed I had a concept that could work. I had already written some spoken verse which depicted my life story. And although my knowledge of PowerPoint was limited, I felt almost certain that if I was to combine my verse with visuals, this would be the difference I was looking for.

This was going to create a far more interesting and innovative talk. Never one for making things easy for myself, I bought a second-hand PowerPoint projector and set about brushing up on the minimal PowerPoint skills I had.

So, in September 2013, having had the privilege of Paul's help and expertise, I officially set up as a sole trader. I started working under the name S.M. Toni, having read somewhere that most successful authors have initials as their first names, such as J.K. Rowling. Mum came up with the idea of S.M. Toni, which was a combination of close family names.

A small local design company created my website while I set about producing social media pages. It did seem a bit more difficult to promote myself rather than confectionery and travel accessories; nevertheless, I put my years of sales experience to good use and booked myself several speaking slots. I'd started getting involved voluntarily with a few mental health charities, so I couldn't be happier when Derbyshire Mind asked me to headline one of their events.

Standing in front of an 80-strong audience at their Discover to Recover event was extremely daunting. My hands were sticky, my mouth was dry, and my heart was beating quite loudly. But this wasn't the start of a panic attack; this was stage fright. I knew that for the following two hours all eyes were on me, and for the first few seconds I couldn't help worrying about all the things that could go wrong. What if the projector failed, what if I forgot what I wanted to say? What if, what if, what if ...

There is some advice that you never forget. I clung onto one piece of valuable advice, and it sprang to mind in those first few seconds. A sales trainer had given it to me during my confectionery-selling days. He'd said, 'If you don't feel scared when you're about to deliver an important presentation, then you cannot be passionate enough about a successful result.'

I was completely overcome by the positive response and feedback I received after the event. One gentleman's reaction has stuck firmly in my mind. He was a taxi driver, and his curiosity had got the better of him after he'd dropped someone off at the football club. His passenger told him what the talk was about, so he'd parked up his cab, sneaked into the hall and found a seat towards the back. Most of the audience had signed up but it was a free event, open to anyone who wished to attend.

Halfway through the talk – during a refreshment break – I went outside for some fresh air. A cab pulled up outside the building and beckoned me over. It was the taxi driver.

'I just wanted to let you know that that was brilliant, and I only wish I could stay for the second half,' he told me. 'But I've got another fare. Keep up the excellent work!' He then drove off.

Feeling incredibly grateful, I had a lengthy discussion with Mum. We both decided it probably wouldn't do me any harm to go to the media with my story. I was already holding talks and discussing it openly at events, but this would reach out to a much wider audience, hopefully helping many others to overcome their own personal hurdles. And so I set about writing a blog, detailing my life experiences. I submitted my story to countless magazines, press agencies, and journalists.

Patience is always a virtue, and I don't think we practise it nearly enough. This was where I truly learnt never to give up at the first hurdle. I taught myself to live on an exceptionally low budget, while passionately building the foundations of a small business. It tested my strengths and weaknesses, and I soon discovered that self-employment was by no means an easy ride. This time, though, I was much more determined. I overcame – and bounced back from – every single knock back, obstacle, and rejection.

While throwing all my energy into the growth of my new business, I also grasped what was really important to me. I reignited some of my childhood passions. From the age of 11 I loved walking among nature, heading off into the Derbyshire countryside most weekends with my younger brother and a picnic basket.

Somehow, though, these kinds of simple pleasures disappeared as I grew older. But with a country park on my doorstep, there could have been no better time to bring back these forgotten, yet loved, pastimes back into my life.

I'd also been a keen fitness fanatic from the age of about 20, and yet – although I'd tried all the best gyms in the town – I never felt comfortable, preferring to train with the guidance of fitness videos in the privacy of my own home. I loved dancing too, and would quite often enjoy my own personal disco, gyrating, spinning, and twirling for hours to all my favourite sounds. There was no better way for me to burn the calories, and it lifted my mood as well.

Sport, on the other hand, was purely made for watching as far as I was concerned. I hated participating in any competitive game and would do almost anything at school to get out of playing hockey or netball. I forged letters from my parents, suggesting I wasn't well enough to participate in that day's session. I deliberately "forgot" my PE kit. I had all sorts of tricks up my sleeve to avoid the tennis courts or get myself out of long jump practice. I just wasn't good enough. Sometimes I even had to play tennis against a wall, because no one wanted me as a member of their knock-out team.

Once again walking and exercise became firmly fixed into my daily routine. Early-morning hikes, meditation, and Davina McCall and Beverley Callard's fitness videos all played their part in aiding my recovery from depression.

My transformation was nothing short of miraculous.

As well as all this, I was finally acknowledging the importance of the creative gift I had been given. I cherished and nurtured my writing, reaping the rewards from my new business.

Towards the end of 2013, I finally received a response to one of the countless emails I had sent out to the media. An agency told me they were certain that my experiences – specifically the shopping addiction – had all the essential ingredients to interest the national media. They were also impressed with how well the detail had been written. And so, within a few weeks, we struck a deal with *Woman's Own magazine.*

In March 2014 they featured my story. Reading about the true Sharon Bull – and what had gone on behind closed doors – must have come as a complete surprise for those who had known me during those dark times. I'd covered my tracks well during those dreadful years, in particular the latter few, and there was no denying that I could put on an elaborate show.

My story gained huge amounts of interest. Mental health charities and national wellbeing movements contacted me. Various radio stations around Derbyshire, Yorkshire, and East Midlands interviewed me too. I was also finally accepted as a blogger for the Huffington Post, after they'd rejected my submissions for 18 months. Here was another reason never to give up and to always have hope.

I gave out good vibes to those who needed some cheer. I listened to those who wanted to offload their anger or frustrations, and offered a shoulder to cry on to anyone wanting some consolation. I took the same stance as my dear late father, believing wholeheartedly his words. 'There is always someone worse off than yourself.'

It was a late sunny afternoon in October 2014 when I skipped out of my new doctor's surgery, almost feeling like a teenager. I'd been given an excellent bill of health, and I had every reason to radiate joy. It was only four years earlier that fast food such as pizzas and crisps – washed down with a couple of bottles of wine – had been my staple diet. My lifestyle had been fuelled by adrenaline, stress, and frustration. I'd given up on my fitness regime and depended entirely on Prozac. My unhealthy habits had become excessive between 2009 and 2011. For all these reasons, I'd felt sure I was going to be delivered some bad news about my internal organs.

I'd breezed through my midlife medical MOT. Other than my lifestyle changes, what else had changed over the past few years?

Firstly, I was no longer under continuous pressure to achieve targets, from either a manager – who had cared little about my wellbeing – or from myself. I was no longer setting myself outrageous, unachievable objectives.

In the eighties a friend once said to me, 'You'll never have a weight problem. You're always on the go!' I'd proved her wrong many years later, but I do understand what she meant. Although I'd always tried to make time for family and friends, generally work and the ongoing quest to improve my status always took precedence.

Secondly, I'd replaced my pursuit of materialism with childhood passions and moral values. It had changed me drastically. I now much preferred to spend my leisure time walking along a quiet lakeside, rather than drowning in the hustle and bustle of a busy department store. I no longer wanted to be seen in the swanky wine bars, trying to stay upright in six-inch heels. Now I wanted to stroll along a beach, feeling the sand between my toes.

Thirdly, I'd decided to become vegetarian in February 2014. The increase in my vitality and spirit was unquestionable. It hadn't been a particularly hard decision to make, because lamb, duck, and rabbit were never part of my diet, and I'd barely eaten red meat for years. The choice to stop eating animals was quite simply due to my concern with the increasing cruelty linked to factory farming.

The food industry seems clouded by the ongoing, intense competition between supermarkets, who want to win over consumers at whatever cost. With total disregard to the animals in their food chain, they feed the greedy bosses and investors with more profit, allowing immoral and inhumane practices to produce meat for the shelves.

Some people may not be so concerned about this, but if we also take into consideration society's growing gluttony – particularly in the western world – and the countless chronic illnesses it causes, then the lining of their pockets also comes at the cost of human life. My conscience could no longer allow me to contribute to another living being's unnecessary suffering.

Lastly, my daily meditation had clearly played a crucial part in my wellbeing. Since May 2012 – apart from the odd day here and there – I had been determined to keep up the discipline. The benefits to my mind alone were amazing, but the results from my midlife MOT were also a testament to its powerful effects on the body.

In late 2014, I came to the conclusion that I needed to change my public speaking name, S.M. Toni. I received a constant barrage of questions about it, and it caused a lot of confusion. They wanted to know the reason behind my decision and how it linked to my talks.

At the time I'd been running an animal welfare petition, and it wasn't particularly successful. But from the frustration and anguish over a failing campaign came the new title for my public speaking and writing business. The campaign had been called A Compassionate Voice, and so I decided to name my business this instead. This was when everything started to move so much faster.

I had a new website created, one that I could maintain myself and to which I could add blogs and videos of my work. My Facebook page – which had just over 500 followers and had been steadily ticking along with little interaction – suddenly gained momentum. Five hundred followers soon became a thousand. As the numbers grew, my verse and blogs continued to reach out to wider audiences, receiving overwhelming feedback and response.

A Compassionate Voice was a business name that finally made sense to everyone.

I toasted in the new year with Jools Holland and his Rhythm & Blues Orchestra at the annual BBC New Year's Eve Hootenanny. I danced into 2015 like I hadn't danced in years. I had so much to be grateful for and everything to look forward to. I don't think there could have been a better way to welcome in the new year.

For the first time in my life, it felt as though I was sitting on top of the world. I no longer needed people to look up to me, applaud my position, or admire me. Instead, I wanted to inspire people, to encourage people to join me in what I had found to be a far better place to dwell.

CHAPTER 13

commuter time

During my 15 years as a travelling salesperson, I clocked up a lot of hours sitting in my car going nowhere. Congestion on motorways and dual carriageways – often caused by accidents triggering tailbacks for miles – was a daily occurrence. My stress levels were very high as I impatiently drummed my fingers on the steering wheel, worrying about getting to my first appointment on time. I would constantly lean at different angles, trying to see if there were any signs of movement in the endless queue of cars in front of me.

Then, realising the improbability of making the arranged time with my customer, I would chunter to myself about the failures of central government. I'd kick myself for not climbing out of bed half an hour earlier, instead of being grateful for not getting caught up in the accident a few miles ahead.

The irony was that most of my customers were understanding of my predicament and only wished me a continued safe journey. The tension was far worse at the end of a working day, after I'd drunk copious amounts of coffee during client meetings. I relied on caffeine and cigarettes, which I seemed to think were the antidotes for my anxiety.

Friday evenings always seemed to be the worst at commuter time, particularly on the M1 heading home from the south.

The amount of times I have sat within a few miles of junction 29, my gateway to the start of the weekend, grumbling about the status quo! Nothing can be changed in that situation though, when I had already passed the previous junction and was a little short of the motorway services. No amount of whining was going to make any difference.

For me and the many drivers surrounding me, though, complaining did seem to kill some time during what could sometimes be a long, drawn out few hours. I often jokily asked my family and friends what aliens would think of our lifestyles, should they exist. What would they think of our planet at commuter times? What would they think of the United Kingdom in particular, a relatively small island compared to other parts of the world? Would they sit in their space crafts and watch us with amusement? Those humanoids, sitting in their metal boxes of varying sizes and colours, going absolutely nowhere!

After my car crash on the M56 I was involved in one or two more traffic accidents, though none were quite as major as the first. I also had a few nerve-wracking experiences triggered by road rage.

Road rage always seemed just around a corner, particularly during rush hour. Tensions would flare at a moment's notice. I wasn't innocent of the two-fingered salute or the odd sudden temper attack either. It was also funny watching some men – who seconds ago were munching their way through breakfast in the middle lane of the motorway – overtaking me, the blonde woman, who had just dared to pass them in her Toyota Avensis. Their testosterone levels were obviously calling the shots!

The scariest incident for me, though, took place on the M6 motorway approaching Lancaster. I was on my way to a visit with a couple of clients. The roadway was almost empty and a solitary officer in his police patrol car must have wanted to spice up his morning. Unfortunately, I was in the wrong place at the wrong time and I became the victim of his fun. For a couple of miles he taunted me as he deliberately moved his vehicle in a laboured manner along the inside lane, only to speed up when I tried to overtake. I remembered the satisfied leer across his face when I pulled back behind him. Once again, he slowed his vehicle down to a snail's pace. Once I realised the game he was playing, I crawled along in the same manner, feeling both frightened and intimidated.

To think that a member of the law, who was there to protect society, could be capable of such harassment was disturbing and scary. I cannot express the relief I felt when my exit came into view. As he noticed me indicate to come off the motorway, he quickly collected his speed and within seconds he'd disappeared over the horizon. His menacing game was over.

I did consider reporting him, but rightly or wrongly I made the decision not to. It was his word against mine and without any witnesses, I felt it would be a difficult one to prove.

I had another equally hair-raising experience on the M1. The consequences could have been horrifying if the circumstances had been different. The M1 was the key motorway for me, the link to most of my territory. The majority of days were spent either heading north or south along its carriageways, and this early morning was no exception. I had not been driving long when the warning signs began.

I spotted a familiar red triangle depicting a workman with his shovel. It told drivers to expect possible delays. The red cones merged three lanes into two as they blocked off the outside lane, but because it was still quiet, it didn't make too much of a difference and the traffic was still free flowing. It wasn't quite the morning rush hour yet, so the odd vehicle approaching the motorway from the following junction wasn't causing any issues yet either. As I passed the junction, I glanced through my rear-view mirror and noticed a car speeding down its slip road. I watched in horror as the driver recklessly steered his car across all three lanes of the motorway. He even carried on driving for a moment or two after plunging through the cones. His dangerous antics could have cost lives, but miraculously for him there was no workforce around. There were just a couple of traffic police in their patrol car who, like me, had obviously seen the entire mindless incident.

I use the word mindless because that's exactly what it was. I can fully appreciate how easy it is to switch on to autopilot, particularly when driving. Through repetition we grow complacent, and our thoughts drift elsewhere. It is something I have been guilty of myself, but shouldn't we be worried when we've driven our vehicle from A to B, without remembering big chunks of the journey? I would say there is a definite argument here: training the mind to live in the present moment is not only better for our health, and it not only helps to reduce tension and anger outbursts, but it also makes us much safer.

These days I don't drive nearly half as much as I used to, but I still know how hard it is to stay calm and courteous when another driver's actions seem inconsiderate.

On returning home from a recent shopping trip with Mum, my patience was tested on the road. I was driving down a stretch of road with cars parked on either side, so I gave way to some oncoming vehicles. Noticing a gap in the flow of traffic coming towards me, I edged my Peugeot 207 forward, only to be faced head on by a ginormous four-by-four. Where the vehicle had sprung from I have no idea, but I soon felt the wrath of its driver.

With no consideration whatsoever, he selfishly forced his way between the parked cars, almost skimming the paint from the side of mine in the process. His face was red and screwed up, and he glared at me through his side window.

'F**k off!' he bellowed at me. A woman was sitting nonchalantly beside him.

Years ago, I would have most definitely responded with a middle finger salute. But not this time. Instead, Mum and I looked at one another and, with grins from ear to ear, we simply screamed, 'BUBBLES!'

"Bubbles" is one of the few words that cannot be said angrily. It's a concept I used for an exercise during my earlier talks. Most members of the audience seemed to love the idea, and "bubbles" soon became my signature word. In moments of provocation or annoyance, shouting 'bubbles!' can seriously change the mood! Go on, try it next time there is a need for it.

There's a lot to be said about a calmer mind, especially during commuting. Surely we'd have safer roads and a reduction in traffic accidents. Mistakes are so often caused by frustrated drivers, and I know this well from my commuting days. Using the word "bubbles" rather than the two-fingered salute would definitely have lightened the mood in my times of anger and frustration.

Mindlessness isn't just confined to road travel, though.

By autumn 2014 I was becoming a regular guest on several local radio stations. It was nearing teatime when I boarded the train back home, after a mid-afternoon interview, and I hadn't booked a particular seat because the journey home was quite short. I didn't think the 30-minute ride warranted the additional stress. I'm sure I'm not alone when I say I've walked up and down carriages a number of times, scrutinising seat numbers only to find someone already sitting in the reserved seat. I'm never quite sure whether to feel embarrassed for the guilty parties – who, desperate not to make eye contact with anyone, always have their heads conveniently buried in a newspaper or magazine – or to feel cross with them for making themselves feel at home in my reserved seat. Their laptop opened, a half-eaten sandwich and take away coffee already littering the table. Sometimes I just simply avoid the confrontation altogether and look elsewhere.

I managed to find myself a seat quite easily this time, and it wasn't long before I could feel the train moving, starting to make its journey northbound. The head steward announced the buffet car's opening times. For some, it was going to be a two- to three-hour journey before they reached their destination, so I was almost certain that the announcement would bring a smile to their faces.

But, no. None of my fellow passengers seemed to have tuned in to the head steward's message. Completely disconnected and unaware of the present moment, they were cosseting their mobile phones, laptops, and notepads instead, as if they had just been reunited with a long-lost lover or friend. Some of the travellers were wearing headphones so as to not be disturbed, while others munched on snacks robotically while staring at their screens. It was almost impossible not to notice the glazed, almost hypnotised looks upon their faces. They were transfixed by their devices. One man ate his way through an entire packet of crisps within barely a minute. I doubt he even tasted them as he shovelled them into his mouth while scrolling through his emails.

'Don't worry, mate. We'll get the deal!' another man said into his phone, boosting his colleague's morale.

The train soon picked up speed, and it wasn't long before we were cutting through the British countryside. On either side of the carriage, a picturesque tapestry filled the windows. There were scenic views of fields, forests, and lakes. It was the height of autumn, but as we passed by nature's priceless splendour and beautiful colours, none of my fellow passengers looked interested. It didn't seem to conjure up any excitement or emotion within them at all.

Most of them were probably wrapped up in this desperate need to succeed. They were all probably preoccupied with that sense of urgency, the feeling that if we don't reach our business targets, sooner rather than later, someone else will beat us to it. Perhaps they were scared that the door of opportunity would be slammed shut forever.

I couldn't help but remember past train journeys I had made, returning home from an exhibition or sales conference. Feeling completely exhausted, I would settle into my seat and instantly start formulating my next set of strategies for success. I thought there was no time to relax my mind. I needed to come up with a master plan, one that would help me take the next step up the prosperity ladder.

Suddenly I felt incredibly sad, realising that most of the commuters sitting around me were almost certainly in this mode. Many of them were probably deliberating, assessing, and conjuring up ways for their next triumphant venture – one that would clarify just how important they were within their business. It's likely that they were totally unaware of their subservience to their egos; ignorant, just as I was, of the importance of living life to the full and the irrelevance of accolades and material possessions.

I wanted to stand up, point to the trees and shout, 'Look at the magnificent colours! Isn't life amazing?' But I doubt anyone would have acknowledged me. And if they had, they would most definitely have thought I was bonkers.

I thought of a quote by Ellen Goodman: "Normal is getting dressed in clothes that you buy for work, driving through traffic in a car that you are still paying for, in order to get to a job that you need so you can pay for the clothes, car, and the house that you leave empty all day in order to afford to live in it."

Over the years, I have regularly talked about the freedom I get when I'm behind the wheel. I didn't pass my driving test until my late twenties, and although my first few ventures out in my old black Opel Manta sports car were daunting, I have never looked back since. Owning a full driving licence opened many new doors for me – ones that would have been permanently closed otherwise. I don't miss the monotony of daily motorway commuting, though, and these days I much prefer to hop on a train for lengthier journeys.

I have loved train travel since being a child. For me, it is the most exciting way to get around and I relish in the idea of someday taking a sightseeing trip around some of the world's train lines. I can't think of a better way to capture the various landscapes and natural backdrops of our planet.

Although I can generally choose when and how I travel now, there are still times when I have to drive during busier hours. When that happens, I can feel the tension in the room escalate, and the atmosphere changes. It's not easy trying to approach these situations with a totally different frame of mind. Strokes and heart attacks can be caused by a constant build-up of unnecessary stress, so even though habitual emotions can be hard to stamp out, surely it's worth a try for your own wellbeing.

Looking back, I wish that I spent what I believed to be wasted moments – as I sat for hours waiting in traffic queues or hanging around for delayed public transport – doing something relaxing instead. I should have calmed myself down, rather than poisoning my mind with toxic negativity. I could have listened to soothing music or an audio book, meditated, or undertaken some mindfulness practice when it was safe to do so. I could have even exchanged smiles with other frustrated commuters to alleviate the boredom and annoyance.

Taking the time to relax and acknowledge what was going on around me, even for a short amount of time, would not have hindered my progress in life. Quite the opposite. The extra mind space could have given me the insight and vision for future projects.

I understand, just like when I encountered the rogue policeman in his patrol car, that there are some external factors that we can't always influence. Taking all things into consideration, I think I reacted in the best way possible. I didn't let him indulge in his pathetic game of control. Yes, for a long time afterwards I hated him for his actions. I hated him for the fear he instilled in me, when I should have pitied his behaviour. I should have considered why he felt it necessary to act that way.

At times it's almost impossible not to hate the perpetrators of ill doing, but this is when I think about Alice Hertz-Sommer. She was a truly remarkable woman. I found a video of her on YouTube, and I was blown away by this very special and inspirational lady.

Alice died in February 2014, at age 110. She was the oldest recorded holocaust survivor, surviving the Theresienstadt concentration camp with her son. She was spared because of her musical talent. She was forced to play the piano for the German troops on a regular basis, and although members of her family were killed during the war (including her mum and husband), she never carried any resentment or hatred throughout her life.

If Alice is not the perfect example of how to live a healthy life free of harmful negative emotions, then I don't know who is.

Somehow, we need to learn and understand why we need to do the same as Alice. No one should suffer long-term exploitation or unfairness, but neither should we let these wrongdoers inflict further damage by allowing them to control our thoughts. If we fill our hearts with love for the persecuted – including ourselves – and hope or pray that the wrongdoers see the error of their ways, they will lose their power over our minds. We'll no longer be held to ransom, and we can do something useful in the fight against injustice. As Alice said, 'Never hate the haters. This will only eat your soul.'

Anger, vile words, and venomous actions seriously destroy our spirits. We need to step back and take a few deep breaths in moments of despair. There are many different things in our lives that can cause stress. But if we replace anger and frustration with a calmer frame of mind, the end result benefits everyone.

CHAPTER 14

nature heals

There are two things that happened in my life that brought home what is truly important. Both were significant in helping me decide the path I would eventually take.

The first incident happened not long after I had moved in with Mum. This was when I first met Sammie, one of three swans who lived on the lake in a local country park. She was beautiful, but I didn't think much about our early-morning encounters at first. As time went by, though, she became a close companion and the catalyst for many of the ideas behind A Compassionate Voice.

I'd become an early riser again. I'd never fully appreciated it, nor had I felt that I had the time to enjoy it before. Peeping through the curtains at a new dawn was a completely different experience to what I was used to. Instead of looking out at a tiny garden surrounded by what seemed like a million houses in every direction, I was greeted with scenic views of woodland, fields, and a huge old oak tree.

Mum's bungalow may have been small, but it had its good points too. Wildlife was in abundance. Nuthatches, woodpeckers, tits, and wagtails hovered around the bird feeders. I always scattered some nuts on the pavers underneath them for the squirrels, wood pigeons, blue jays, and robins. We also had the odd visit from a sparrow hawk, though I doubt he was interested in the nuts.

I remember feeling extremely nervous when I went on my first early-morning walk in the country park alone. With no one around, it took me quite some time before I dared go off the beaten track. I was on edge, worrying about how vulnerable I would be in secluded areas. But a part of me desperately wanted to explore.

It had been a long time since I'd embraced the countryside in this way. I was far more used to bustling shopping centre streets.

With each visit, though, the fear subsided. I started to savour every sound. I noticed the different colours in each of the seasons. I walked through rain, snow, wind, and sunshine. I braved new pathways and walked over meadows, even finding small hidden areas where I could spend time practising mindfulness.

I would trudge through the woods at least four or five times a week in my leopard-print wellington boots. In the winter months I'd wrap up in warm layers of clothing underneath a walking jacket, brown woollen scarf, and matching cap. In summer I'd wear tracksuit bottoms and T-shirts. I'd take a bottle of water, a mobile phone, and feed for the wildlife – just the bare essentials – and head off for two hours of peace and tranquillity.

Wandering between the trees, I became blissfully aware of their differences in size and stature. I noticed the robins peering at me through the branches, spotted the squirrels as they quickly scurried out of sight among the branches. Every morning was a completely different adventure, a totally changing picture of natural beauty. I've witnessed the sky so heavy with snow, it seemed to touch a ground already covered in inches of the stuff, creating a white canvas effect. I have been privileged enough to see a mixture of autumn colours so magnificent against a blue sky, it took my breath away. I've seen an eclipse of the sun made even more beautiful by the serenity of the lake and surrounding woodland.

Being among nature is one place I can guarantee anyone can heal, learn to be mindful, and live in the present moment. This was when every book I had read suddenly seemed to make sense. My life suddenly felt as though the last, most important piece of a jigsaw had been found, a piece that had been missing for a very long time.

As time went on, it seemed as though the wildlife was becoming familiar with my presence. Robins would come out to greet me and squirrels didn't automatically go into hiding. I always thought that maybe the reason they did this was the crunching sound of my feet under the crisp snow or on fallen leaves. But in theory this should have given them the opportunity to make themselves scarce.

Is nature's intuition much stronger than ours? Did the robins and squirrels sense kindness and love through my energy and vibrations? I was intrigued, and I started to do some research.

I found an article by Maryann Mott, written not long after the tsunami in 2005. "Did Animals Sense Tsunami Was Coming?" It discussed the behaviour of animals – in particular the wildlife – up to 10 days prior to the natural disaster. It questioned whether it was their intuition that saved so many more of them than human beings.

Sammie the swan was also showing these tendencies too. She seemed to realise who I was immediately. Whenever I approached the lake with feed she would look me straight in the eyes, chatter to me with her beak, and wag her back tail in delight. Eventually she started stepping out of the water to greet me, standing by my side and even tugging at my coat sleeve a few times with her beak. Eventually I overcame my nervousness and allowed her to eat from the palm of my hand. She was a gentle, beautiful bird who not only helped me with my recovery, but – at a crucial point in my life – gave me a sharp reminder of how wonderful for the soul unconditional love can be.

But it wasn't until August 2014 that I realised just how important Sammie had become to me. I hadn't been to the country park for over a week because of a holiday, but on my return I noticed she was in some kind of distress after taking feed from me. Her beak wouldn't close and she seemed to be gagging, almost choking. I was extremely concerned. I walked over to the park ranger's office, but there was no one there, so I called a national animal charity when I got home.

Before I left the park, I passed by the lake to check on Sammie again. The gagging seemed to have stopped and after being assured by a member of the fishing club that a vet was taking care of her injury, I went home relatively happy, thinking there was no need for further concern.

Somehow, though, I just couldn't get Sammie out of mind. I decided to step up my visits to the lake to keep an eye on her. For almost three weeks this beautiful bird suffered unduly because of the faith and trust I put in others. As it turns out, no one was looking after her, and I had an ongoing struggle with the animal charity and some of the fishermen, who used the lake regularly. Both continually discredited my concerns about Sammie. They tried to make me believe that she was in perfect health. But in my mind, there wasn't a shadow of a doubt: Sammie was deteriorating fast.

I spent almost a full day by the lake, taking videos and pictures of the lethargic bird to prove her suffering. Still no one took any notice, so I decided to find help elsewhere. The problem was that I had no idea where to go or who to speak to. I felt completely overwhelmed, powerless, and grief stricken, because although I knew time was running out for my beautiful feathered friend, I couldn't seem to get the help that she needed and deserved.

But at last my determination paid off when an internet search pulled up some smaller wildlife sanctuaries. Within hours Sammie was rescued by the Yorkshire Swan Rescue Hospital.

I was both devastated and relieved when Dan, the charity's founder, told me that she probably wouldn't have lasted much more than a couple of days. If only I'd known about these volunteer rescue charities! I could have spoken to someone so much sooner.

I watched Dan as he lifted her from the water. The cause of her ill health soon became apparent. A discarded fishing line was cutting deep into her lower beak and down her neck, making it almost impossible for her to digest food. For over three weeks this graceful bird had been slowly starving to death under the watchful eye of a few human beings – human beings who didn't want their favourite pastime being marred by any bad publicity. As Dan wrapped a safety harness around her, I gently stroked the top of her head and prayed that it wasn't already too late.

For a little while it was touch and go for Sammie. But the small group of volunteers at the wonderful North Yorkshire Sanctuary slowly managed to bring her back to full health. Just before Sammie's release (she had a three-month recuperation period at Yorkshire Swan Rescue Hospital), I drove up to see my lovely feathered friend. Sadly for me, she barely recognised who I was. This was the last time I ever saw her, because she ended up being released on a lake in Yorkshire, where she could live out the rest of her days more safely.

Sammie taught me so much during those three years. She reignited my passion for helping the vulnerable, while also reminding me who I truly was. I will never forget the many precious moments I was fortunate to spend with her. My own personal issues were completely obliterated during my determined efforts to save her life. Sammie was equally essential in saving my life too, so I was desperately happy that I could repay her during her time of need.

To find out more about Yorkshire Swan Rescue Hospital please visit **www.ysrh.org.uk**

CHAPTER 15

cry for help

'If someone had told me a few years ago that I would be speaking in Trafalgar Square at a peaceful demonstration, I wouldn't have believed them,' I began my speech. 'I've loved animals since being a child. I'd watch the cowboy films with my dad, and when the fights broke out with the Indians I'd say, "I hope none of the horses get hurt!"

'The thing is, for years I've been marching through life trying to be this person I thought I was supposed to be – to be seen as successful. It wasn't until unexpected events turned my life upside down that I realised the world I was living in was a sham. And that's when I woke up to who I really was!

'What I am trying to say is that people and circumstances change. That's why we are here today – to raise awareness and encourage the change.'

It was Saturday, January 17th 2015 and I'd joined over a thousand people in London's winter sunshine. We were helping to raise awareness about the truth behind dolphin and whale captivity.

The peaceful demonstration encouraged a wide variety of protesters. There were young people, old people, families, children, teenagers, and pets. Some were in fancy dress, but all were in good spirits as we made our way to Trafalgar Square with a message to share. We were compassionate, caring people, ring-fenced by various labels created by leaders in order to protect their domains.

So often movements and groups are said to represent a minority opinion, when in actual fact statistics clearly show that they speak on behalf of the majority of the public.

January 17th was also the first anniversary of the capture of Angel, a rare baby albino dolphin who, along with Sammie the swan, had captured my heart. Angel became another kingpin of A Compassionate Voice.

I have loved dolphins since I was a child. For many years, swimming with these beautiful creatures had been on my bucket list, nestled in between witnessing the Northern Lights and travelling on the Orient Express. Sadly, in my ignorance, I failed to question how these dolphins ended up in captivity, until January 2014 when I witnessed the cruel kidnapping of Angel. Swimming innocently by the side of her mother, she was callously ripped from the sea in Taiji, Japan, and taken for a life of captivity. Just like many more dolphins around the world, she was taken from her natural habitat to fuel a trade that profited from yet another form of animal abuse.

My heart broke into a million pieces when I learnt of the extreme pain, anxiety, and suffering that these endearing, sentient beings endured, just to humour people at dolphin shows. Their natural playfulness was exploited to line the pockets of a few. Once again this was proof that I needed to give my voice to the voiceless, so it was a proud moment for me to speak on their behalf in Trafalgar Square.

While reciting my poem *Message from an Angel,* I became completely overwhelmed. Looking out across Trafalgar Square, listening to the deafening silence that fell upon the crowd as I delivered Angel's message over the microphone, I watched many of the onlookers reaching for their hankies. It suddenly became apparent to me that I could help raise awareness through my written work. I had penned the poem a few days after Angel's capture, in the hope it would reach out to mums and dads who were maybe contemplating taking their children to a dolphin show.

Surely my creativity could speak out for many other issues and injustices too.

I have never questioned my love for every living creature I share the planet with, whether it is a tiny spotted ladybird or the most majestic of elephants. But like many more, I have lived in ignorance for a long time about the immense cruelty bestowed upon living beings throughout the world.

It takes education, research, and understanding before embarking on a crusade, but like a dog with a bone, I will never be shaken from what I truly believe is my purpose in life. My intentions are set in stone: I will do whatever I can – wherever I am able – to help the vulnerable and the voiceless.

I am ashamed of humanity's lack of respect for animals and other living beings. What I have witnessed through live streams and pictures on social media over the past few years is beyond cruel, and in the 21st century it's simply not justified. Pilot whales are held hostage for days in shallow waters, left without food before meeting a grisly death. Thousands of farm animals are transported for days in cramped conditions without access to basic comforts, just to be slaughtered at the end of their harrowing journey. Bears are captured and caged for up to 15 years to produce medicinal bile, and beagle puppies are raised purely for experimentation. Some never see the outdoors; some are unable to smell the fresh air or feel the warmth of the sun on their backs. They are ripped from their families and denied even the smallest grain of happiness. Factory farming, dolphinariums, bull fighting, trophy hunting – the list is endless. It's all animal exploitation, driven by a small minority's thirst for greed and power.

The treatment of some animals is a sickening outrage. They are all prisoners who have been served a death sentence, having done nothing wrong. They are born without a voice.

I gave another speech on 16th January, 2016 during a protest in support of dolphins, opposing their slaughter and captivity.

'To the Taiji fishermen, the Japanese government, the British government and all the powers that be – those of you who continue to turn your backs on the inexcusable violent crimes bestowed upon other living beings. I am going to ask you all, just for a few moments, to change places with the dolphin that I witnessed in the video recently. I want you to try to imagine that these are the last few precious moments of your life, or maybe even your child's life. Or any of your family's lives. As a conscious, sentient being, just like the dolphin in the video, I want you to imagine that during those last moments, someone callously and repeatedly stamps and kicks at your head without compassion or remorse. Someone who obviously deems your life to be worthless and makes this clear to you right until the bitter end. Now, please try to explain why these evil crimes against nature are still being allowed to continue.'

We claim to be the most intelligent species in the world. Ironically, though, we have christened ourselves with this particular crown. If other living beings could speak in our tongue, I doubt they would agree. And who could blame them either? Our minds may be superior, but we only have to look at our behaviour towards each other – the disrespect we show for other life forms and the disregard we show for Mother Earth – to realise that we have misinterpreted our purpose for being here.

Greed and the accumulation of possessions and power seem to be the driving force behind many of humankind's decisions. They encourage the most despicable trades around the world. Freedom was meant for all, and no matter how much wealth we amass from the exploitation of animals.

Just like them, we enter this world alone with nothing. And we will also die alone, taking with us absolutely nothing.

There have been a number of times when I've sat with my pet cat, Maddie, sharing with her my thoughts and ideas. I've mulled over problems with her. She's been content with me during good times and bad times, through tears of joy and sadness. Never has she complained or told me to shut up when I've been telling her my latest dramas! Sometimes she might have walked away in her cat-like manner, with her nose and tail pointed towards the ceiling, but, more often than not, her big blue eyes were fixated on me as she listened to my every word.

Like all animals, she is unable to speak to me. And yet Maddie has found many ways to communicate with her human family, so I fail to understand why anyone would underestimate an animal's level of intelligence – or worse, deny they have feelings. I am sure most pet owners will agree that our fur babies become a cherished part of the family. Even though they don't have voices, we can usually tell by their behaviour if they are happy, sad, or unwell.

Most pet owners appreciate that their dogs and cats have intelligent little minds. During one of my early-morning strolls, I overheard a conversation. Two elderly people were walking their dogs through the woods. 'He almost talks to me. He understands every word I say,' one said to the other.

'I know. Mine's exactly the same. He seems to know when I'm not feeling well, too,' the other replied.

I had already discovered from Sammie and some of the other wildlife inhabitants in the country park that they too have incredible intelligence, but not only this, they are also probably more intuitive than perhaps we are. What about farm animals, though, who are so often painted to be stupid with neither intelligence nor emotion?

You can clearly tell how much we love animals on social media too. They're even more popular on there than celebrities are.

They are the true superstars of the internet. There is little doubt that most humans cherish animals, or at least wouldn't wish unnecessary suffering on them.

So why are they dealt such a cruel disservice all over the world? Because far too many decisions are made with the mind – to feed the ego – rather than from the heart. We need to help turn this around.

H. Jackson Brown Jr once said, 'Our character is what we do when we think no one is looking.' When I was a little girl, I used to pick up worms and put them out of harm's way, somewhere the birds couldn't see them, and where they wouldn't be trodden on. I was besotted with nature, enchanted by the beauty I saw in all life forms.

I have a little secret I would like to share with you. I still pick up worms today and put them out of harm's way. It's not because I'm eccentric or unbalanced, but because that particular action comes from my heart. It's not driven by the ego. I'm not expecting the worm to turn around and say, 'Hey, thank you for that, what can I give you back in return?' In this instance I am connecting with who I am.

I decided in early 2015 to visit a sanctuary for farm animals, because I needed to witness first-hand what I knew to be right in my heart. I had plucked "Woolly Farm" from a long list of animal rescue charities unearthed by a Google search, because of the founder's dedication to sheep and lambs. I had been a vegetarian for just over a year, and I was already starting to replace some dairy products with plant-based alternatives. It was so much easier than I had imagined to buy vegan products from high-street stores. They tasted just as nice and were equally as nutritious. My switch in diet was long overdue, because anything else was a complete contradiction to my personal moral values. I'd refused to eat lamb since I was a little girl. That had to be an indication of who I truly was.

Tests seem to have proven that pigs share a similar intelligence level to other species that are credited for their intellect, such as dogs, chimpanzees, elephants, and dolphins. But what about sheep, chickens, turkeys, and goats?

Should intelligence define a species' value, anyway? They all feel happiness, love, and fear. Surely the fact that they are born with a beating heart is the only thing that matters.

Having lived on the edge of the Derbyshire Peak District for more than 50 years, I have seen countless lambs joyfully frolicking with their siblings and mothers. Excursions, family holidays to Blackpool, visits to relatives in Lancashire, head-office meetings, and business trips – they were all made extra special when I saw the sight of innocence and new life. I can't bear to think about what little time these delightful creatures have before they are separated from their family. I hate to imagine their fear as they huddle together for comfort, being driven to their final destination.

I regularly visited Farm Animal Rescue Sanctuary (Woolly Farm). I felt absolute joy when I bottle fed rescued lambs. I felt sheer delight when my favourite ram, Joey, ran across the field to join me after hearing me call out his name. He would nudge me affectionately for his favourite treats, knowing I never came to the sanctuary empty handed.

The sanctuary was a humanitarian haven away from the media and technology madness. It was far more relaxing than any weekend spa break. Besides, it also included a free facial and body mud pack delivered by a six-month-old pig named George!

Over recent years I have been fortunate enough to continue meeting animals at sanctuaries. It's only ever reaffirmed what I know to be true. All sentient beings want to be happy; all sentient beings want to feel loved. Most importantly, all sentient beings want to live.

These sanctuaries are not only heaven on earth for the rescued animals. For me, they are wonderful retreats. They are places of tranquillity, where devotion to a cause leads the way and my personal wellbeing is revitalised.

'But there are so many injustices to human beings in the world, too!' I might hear you scream. You are right. One of the organisers of the protest I attended was asked a similar question. 'Why dolphins? Surely there are many more important issues around the world to protest about?'

Her response was poignant, and it resonates with me completely. She suggested to the person that whatever their concerns – whatever felt important to them – change could only be triggered by actively doing something to effect it.

And so this is my passion, knitted together with a strong commitment to helping disadvantaged children. My future plans have never been more purposeful.

So, I would like to make a proposal. Whatever you feel most passionate about – no matter how many people say you are wrong, and regardless of how many people sneer or laugh behind your back – do it. If it feels like the right thing to do and it's going to make a positive difference, then do it.

Too many people do absolutely nothing, simply because they think that as an individual they have little power to make a difference. But if everyone made a few tiny changes and took positive steps towards altering their lifestyles for the benefit of others and the planet, the impact would be significant. We cannot afford to leave things to everyone else. We must grab what is important to us with both hands and do something today. That way we can guarantee a much better world to live in.

Do we really want to go down in the history books as the generation that screwed things up?

Since 2012 I have been privileged to witness so much positivity.

I have watched seven fluffy little ducklings grow up, nervously counting them one by one on every visit, grateful none of them had come to any harm. I've seen talented air displays as seagulls playfully swooped down for bread. I've shared time with a robin in a secluded woody area, watching him enjoy the seed I had gently placed on the branch. He seemed to pose for my new camera as I desperately tried to work out the settings. I've chattered with squirrels when they've stopped to give me the once over, before scurrying across out of sight.

I have enjoyed the autumn winds blowing across the lake's water, creating ripples on the surface. I've felt the cool air also sweep gently across my face. From my favourite park bench, I've watched the ducks and geese go about their daily business. I've giggled at the swan gliding towards them like royalty. I've jumped in muddy puddles, written in the snow and screamed 'life is wonderful!' from a deserted hilltop.

Nature has been profound in my healing. But whenever I walk, sit, or meditate while surrounded by its beauty, it's also a constant reminder to me that we are never truly alone.

We should always stick by what we consider to be morally right, even if sometimes it feels like we are standing alone.

To find out more about Farm Animal Rescue Sanctuary please visit **www.farmanimalrescue.org.uk**

CHAPTER 16

a new breed of politician

Ashamedly, I had very little interest in politics until a few years ago. I have voted in most elections, but only because I remembered my dad's harsh tones the one time I didn't.

'What's the point?' I sheepishly said to him. 'MPs are all the same!'

I admit to feeling despair, though, after hearing the final UK election result during the summer of 2015. For many years I couldn't have cared less which party was governing the country, but I couldn't help but nod my head in agreement when I read the headline news that day.

"FIVE MORE DAMNED YEARS" printed a national tabloid paper.

In my eyes, the wrong party had won the election. But would any other party have made any difference to my town, to this country? To the world, even? I doubt it. And yet countless times I heard the word "compassion" bandied around in the candidate debates. The fact that it was being used as a means to win hearts was laughable. Compassion was obviously scripted into manifesto pledges, encouraging voters to place a cross against his or her name as each candidate fought for the keys to 10 Downing Street.

Compassion *should* be a key element in political decision making. But it will take more than the word being cleverly manipulated into politicians' speeches to address all the humanitarian issues in the UK, let alone across the world! It's sickening to hear this word being used so flippantly, when we have so many unresolved problems that could have been tackled sympathetically a long time ago.

I watched the critical debate about the war with ISIS (ISIL) intently before parliament cast their vote. I watched a packed House of Commons, busier than I had ever seen it before. As a nation we have very little to be proud of, with so many children living in poverty, families struggling to pay their bills, an NHS crying out for funding, visits to foodbanks at a record high, homelessness on the increase, and a substantial growth in mental health problems. These are all important matters that have been escalating for a number of years, but somehow they have never been shown the same level of importance – or support – as the possibility of war.

I listened to the jeering, the cheering, the flamboyant speeches, some riddled with propaganda and others that did nothing but feed some of the MP's inflated egos. It confirmed to me just how desperately in need of a new breed of politician this world is.

History repeated itself once more as the vote was cast to go to war, despite the growing concern of the public. They seemed to reach a conclusion without time to take a breath, barely allowing anyone even a moment to think things through clearly. It was a swift kneejerk reaction that will once again inevitably put more lives in danger. As Albert Einstein said, the definition of insanity is doing the same thing over and over again and expecting different results.

My point is that compassion must rank high on any agenda, pushing aside power, wealth, and status.

In my mind, selfishness was described perfectly by the Dalai Lama on World Peace Day – 21st September 2015 – when I was fortunate enough to see him speak at an event held in the London Lyceum. The national movement Action for Happiness was running the event. I will try to explain, in my own words, his concept of the two types of selfish: wise selfish and foolish selfish.

"Foolish selfish" is all about me, me, me. It has no consideration for others. Combined with greed and power, it will encourage exploitation, deceit, and corruption. In the worst-case scenario, this type of insensitive, self-seeking lifestyle can also inflict suffering, harm, or ultimately death to others. There is never a good outcome from this type of selfishness. If it is used as a motive to succeed, it will only ever give short-term satisfaction.

"Wise selfish", on the other hand, is a much less complicated way to live. Although we must learn to love ourselves, we do it so that we have the strength, understanding, and empathy to help others.

As individuals, we are all capable of being foolish selfish. But we can also practise wise selfish too. We can get rid of some of our habits, actions, and impulses that encourage the foolish selfish to take a lead role.

I truly believe that there is already an outpouring of "wise selfish" throughout the world. I reckon the intensity in kindness is growing, prompted by the increase in awareness of the many injustices and unnecessary sufferings of all living beings. This gives me so much hope for the future, overshadowing any pessimism I have about decisions made by politicians, or world leaders.

Are we seeing the shoots of change from the multitudes of people doing wonderful things? There are campaigners, volunteers, activists, defenders, do-gooders, philanthropists, Good Samaritans. These are the real advocates of compassion.

In the past the headline "From Addict to Activist" has been used to describe my transformation from shopping addict to campaigner. Although I wouldn't argue with its illustration of my journey so far, in truth there have been many other facets to my renewed lifestyle.

But one of the best ways I feel able to explain my life up to the present date is by describing it as having lived on either side of a fence. I feel fortunate for being given the opportunity to have experienced both sides. It's a shame that due to my reluctance to cross over onto the other side, it took 30 years to do so.

There are many reasons why people dare not venture onto the other side of the fence: fear of the unknown, fear of leaving behind comfortable lifestyles, fear of who we will become, even the fear of losing our identity.

Sadly, for so long I was guided by "foolish selfish". I thought it was the right place to be. Therefore, my life was swamped with delusion, turmoil, depression, and disappointment. I can ill afford to say that my time on the first side was wasted though, because this is where I have spent the biggest chunk of my life so far. The wisdom I've gained from these harsh life lessons is invaluable.

I now find it extremely difficult to understand why I hung around on the first side for so long. What was I doing? What was I thinking? What was it I waiting for? A knight in shining armour, perhaps? Did I want to prove my psychiatrist wrong? Did I want to win six numbers on the lottery?

None of these things would have made me any happier at the time.

But this is why I believe that activism and political movements are spreading like wildfire – because people like me are constantly waking up and crossing over onto the other side of the fence. They've realised that life on the first side wasn't all it was cracked up to be.

Some may come to the realisation much sooner than others, and others – like me – will take a while longer. But as the masses grow, so will the encouragement, until even those sitting on the fence will climb down, unable to bury their heads any longer.

This is how we will effect positive changes in the world and in our own lives – when we unite to put things right and influence a new breed of politician.

CHAPTER 17

the lessons i've learnt

There were times I found writing this book extremely tough. It almost felt as though I was living and breathing my past experiences once again. But it was also good for me, too. In many ways, it helped me fathom out where I was going wrong. I finally grasped that I had been holding myself back in my thought processes, which then consequently affected my actions.

During the last two years, I have spoken to a wide range of audiences and reached out to thousands of people through my written work. As an inspirational speaker, author and poet, I have been privileged to share the issues that are extremely close to my heart, such as mental health recovery, stigma, wellbeing and animal welfare.

But my journey is far from over. Knowing there is a purpose in what I do gives me great courage to push ahead, overcoming any obstacles and leaving behind all the stuff I once thought of as important. I have blamed others for my own unhappiness, possibly brought people into my life, who like me, were suffering from their own delusions, but to accuse anyone for my own negative outlook on life was wrong.

Helping others and raising awareness through the written and spoken word has turned my life around. I know now that I have a purpose. I know that I'm the person I want to be, not who I think

I should be in order to fit into society or make others happy. This has been key to maintaining my mental and physical wellbeing.

At the end of an event in late 2013, a lady came up to me and whispered in my ear, 'That was brilliant because you are real.' This was one of the biggest compliments anyone could have paid me, and thankfully I've heard it many times since. I'm real because I am completely open about my fears, fears of the type that most people sweep under the carpet in the hope that they will either disappear or resolve themselves. That fear results in people making the same mistakes over and over again, because they are too scared to roll back the carpet and face them head on.

Being "real" can be extremely difficult at times, especially with people who have wronged me, so I can honestly say with my hand on heart that I don't always get it right. But while ever my heart is still beating – and no matter what obstacles I must overcome – I will continue to speak out for mental health issues, the disadvantaged, the voiceless and the environment.

I know the type of world I want to live in, and I am almost certain that the vast majority of us have the same dream. I also know that it'd take a huge miracle to overturn centuries old traditions, beliefs and ideas. But – as I am sure readers of this book will have already guessed – I do believe miracles are possible.

Below are a number of life lessons that I've learnt during my first half-century and beyond.

Unity is strength, and compassion is everything.

Through making more mindful and compassionate choices in our lives, we can create a ripple effect that can touch not only those around us, but thousands of others too. Never underestimate the power we all have to create a better world – because even if we don't see effective changes in our own lifetimes, it shouldn't stop us from getting the ball rolling.

My faith in humanity does crumble a little when I hear about movements, charities and organisations who are all working towards the same positive goal and yet seem reluctant to join forces. Perhaps they're stifled by in-house politics, slight differences in opinion, jealousy or – even worse – clashes caused by ego (this seems to be the predominant cause of so many breakdowns in communication). But for me, unity is our only strength, and unless the majority cast aside their disputes and pull together, the perpetrators of corruption and immorality will keep the upper hand.

There is only one answer: we must join hands and work together to achieve compassion, happiness and peace.

Everyone should do what they can in their own way – whichever feels most comfortable. Most importantly, you should do it when the time seems appropriate. Perhaps not everyone will get to see your point of view, but if you take positive steps others will be inspired to follow.

I truly believe that the world would be a much better place if we were more open with each other, if we judged less and showed more compassion – firstly to ourselves, and then to others. We should all work together and use our unique talents to counteract other's weaknesses. My past experiences seem to back up the "like attracts like" theory very strongly. In other words, our lives are simply a mirror image of how we feel about ourselves. We pull into life what we project outwards.

Strength can be gained from hardship and pain, and we can't always have what we want.

My earliest recollection of envy was as a small child, when my cousin came to visit with her family over the Christmas holidays. Santa had left her the first walking, talking doll under their Christmas tree and I was devastated that I had not received one too. With teary eyes, I watched her proudly demonstrate the expensive toy's skills, wondering what I could have possibly done to upset Mr Claus. He had left me some wonderful presents, but not this beautiful, clever doll.

It's not always easy for small children to understand the reasons behind certain situations, but when my elder cousin saw a tear trickling down my cheek, she beckoned me over to play with her new toy.

As adults, though, we must come to terms with the fact that we cannot always have everything we want – no matter how unjust it may seem. Even if you think you've been dealt the short straw, demonising the world isn't the answer. Instead, it's good to try to understand why it wasn't meant to be. Besides, there are probably a million and one alternatives that work out better for us in the long run.

Truthfully speaking, my share of disappointments is still equal to my achievements. But whatever the circumstance, I am more driven than ever before, often motivated by setbacks to work even harder. I can't afford to wallow in self-pity for too long.

So, before you give up hope, remember that we all must be prepared to struggle occasionally. Listen to your heart for guidance and you'll achieve your goals in a fair and honest manner.

We have to face up to our fears and make our own choices. We cannot hide or run away from them.

In 1999 I stopped my 20-a-day smoking habit. The reason for my decision? I'd simply had enough.

Since the age of 14, after I'd shared a few crafty puffs on one of Dad's flipped cigarettes with my brother, the nicotine dependency had taken hold. It kept me hooked for almost 25 years. I started with packets of No 6 and then moved onto Benson & Hedges. I even spent a short period of time trying to master the art of rolling my own, buying cigarette papers and loose tobacco. But somehow, I never quite grasped the technique. I was all fingers and thumbs.

I was on a train journey down to London to see my favourite band Squeeze when I decided to make things simple again and bought a packet of 20 cigarettes. A young guy had been watching me frantically battle with paper and loose tobacco. The motion of the train was making it even more difficult than normal. Smiling, he asked me if he could help. Within seconds he had rolled it, sealed it and handed it back. It was a perfectly even looking tobacco joint. I'd never once managed to accomplish that. Feeling a little peeved, I thanked him and graciously accepted his offer of a light as well.

At some point I inhaled a milder brand for a few years, believing this would be better for my health. But eventually I brought the curtain down on my addiction.

I had tried a few times to quit, but obviously I didn't want it badly enough, because the slightest upset would find me reaching for an unopened packet, hidden away in a handbag. Sometimes, in desperation, I'd rush to the nearest local shop to stock up.

Often people think that it will help to relieve our burdens if we comfort ourselves with addictive and often destructive habits such as smoking, overeating, drinking, taking drugs, gambling, or – in my case – spending.

But all these short-term pleasures actually do is dull the way we truly feel for a short period of time.

They keep our focus preoccupied on the nonsense. They stop us trying to find the root cause of our tattered emotions. Although sometimes it seems easier this way, sadly our problems never go away if we don't face them head on. Problems do have a strange way of developing into huge great whopping complications if, over a long period of time, we deliberately choose to ignore them.

In 1999 I was encouraged to put an end to my nicotine habit. I was fed up with feeling breathless after climbing a few flights of stairs, sick of smelling the lingering stale of tobacco in the car, living room and even sometimes on my clothes. I decided it was time to screw up the fag packet and quit, which is exactly what I did.

It was late one evening and I had been chain smoking during an hour-long phone call with a friend. I put down the receiver and clenched my fist tightly around the cigarette packet. I knew the damage would make the last four filter tips unrepairable, but without any remorse I threw the screwed-up remnants into the kitchen waste bin.

The following morning I did wonder how soon it would be before I purchased another packet. Thankfully, though, from that day on I never smoked again.

Family and friends were astonished at how easily I chucked the £40–£50 a week habit. I never needed nicotine patches or gum. I didn't find it difficult at all – I only ever succumbed to a crafty drag after a few beers with friends a couple of times.

The funny thing is that once I had decided to stop, I never once considered reaching for a smoke – not even during my biggest heartaches, or the most punishing issues. Sometimes I needed alternative habits to get me through, but I should have figured out that my ease in quitting smoking was a clear indication of something. If I wanted a situation to change – if I wanted a different outcome badly enough – then I likely had both the inner strength and the willpower to do it.

Over the years I have been gullible, and I've fallen for many quick-fix solutions sold over the counter, marketed as the easiest way to solve personal flaws. I've spent so much money on anti-aging face cream, cellulite removal cream and weight loss plans. Many of these do work but change takes willpower too.

It's sad, the lack of trust many of us have in our own capabilities. We sustain companies that are dependent on society's weaknesses, and yet a healthy lifestyle can generally be achieved without cost.

We are social beings, so cooperation is needed for survival. Keeping a united front is the only way we will solve the countless troubles we face. But we shouldn't confuse this with being dependent on others for our own wellbeing and happiness either.

It's down to us. No matter how perfect a relationship may be, life can change in an instant. Therefore, it is essential that we have our own inbuilt mechanisms to survive both the ups and the downs. We can seek advice, ask for guidance and read books, but the bottom line is that we must make our own choices in the end. If we let ourselves be guided by peer pressure, bullying, or low self-esteem, I guarantee it'll be the wrong decision.

There are no real shortcuts.

In this modern world of instant gratification, the answer to achieving swift results seems to be to take shortcuts. Time appears to be the biggest fear factor. Sometimes we believe that our goals aren't being met quickly enough, sometimes it's because we're competitive, or worse still, our inflated egos take over.

We also live in a world which seems to expect too much too soon. Patience doesn't seem to be valued enough. This means that often we give up on our dreams so easily and lose heart if we fall at the first hurdle.

But success is generally derived from months – and more often that not, years – of hard work and trial and error.

Always choose love.

During my school days, I jilted someone after our first date. It was purely because of the jumper he wore to meet me. I had swooned over him for months.

How fickle can we be sometimes? Particularly when we are young!

My first love was with the seventies popstar Marc Bolan. I was almost 12 years old and the proud owner of a red and cream record player. I bought the few T Rex 45s I had with the money I earned from my Saturday job, and I played them tirelessly.

One in particular spun around the turntable time and time again, because I genuinely believed that he said my name towards the end of the song. I would move the needle to the right place on the vinyl, just so I could listen to his soft gentle voice say "Sharon".

At 13 my allegiance to the corkscrew-haired singer waned a little, and I drifted towards David Bowie. I also fell for a handsome redcoat at Pwllheli Butlins. I met him on a holiday I was taking with my best friend and her family. We would sit in the camp's grooviest café bar, listening to the latest sounds on the jukebox. 'Life on Mars' was one of our favourites, and to this day the song brings back fond memories of my youth. I was so sad to find out that the café bar was destroyed in a huge fire at the holiday complex not long after we'd left.

We meet so many wonderful people during our journey through life. Sometimes we meet them only fleetingly, yet during that short space of time we often bond with them in a way we never forget.

My friend Marie and I decided to take our very first cruise in the late nineties. It was a last-minute holiday deal, which not only included a week cruising around the Caribbean Islands, but also a week's stay in an all-inclusive hotel on the Dominican Republic. The cruise was an adventure, but our trip offered us so much more – it raised our awareness of other walks of life.

Most of the locals who worked at the hotel had very little in the way of possessions, yet they had such big hearts and were always in high spirits. At the end of our holiday we left the island feeling both privileged and blessed to have been able to share some time with these incredible people. Our suitcases contained the usual souvenirs on the way back, but we also took home with us a little piece of the Dominican Republic; treasured moments that we knew would stay within our hearts forever.

It's no surprise, then, that we were completely traumatised a few months after we returned home, when a hurricane hit the island, causing mass devastation and hundreds of deaths. There was no way of knowing at that time if any of our friends had been killed or displaced. The world seemed a much bigger place then; often countries were solely dependent on news broadcasters to share the details about their plight.

Images of distressed children caught up in war-torn villages are published within seconds across social media. Almost immediately we want to reach out, even when the child is a stranger. This is the essence of love. It defines who we are. We have a desire to help fellow human beings or animals, who can only ever repay us back with their gratitude.

Unconditional love doesn't automatically seek a reward, and it's not steered by social status. It doesn't provoke jealousy or revenge. It's the only answer to a happier, more peaceful and unified world, and it can work perfectly when it isn't clouded by mindless distractions.

Opening our hearts – and choosing love above hate – should take precedence every time.

Choose understanding, not anger.

Over the past few years, meditation and mindfulness have seriously helped to quash my anger. These practices have raised my consciousness levels, so now during times of stress I am more aware of my emotions and how they affect me.

I have never been under any illusions about my own personal vendettas, some of which have been driven by jealousy and envy. Through mindfulness and meditation, I have come to realise that although these feelings are perfectly normal, the danger stems from when I allow them to hang around for too long. These types of emotions can very quickly turn to rage, and they're soul destroying for everyone involved.

I have always hated being backed into a corner, and although I handle these situations very differently now, there was a time when I would respond in mere defiance.

Before successfully quitting smoking, I boycotted restaurants and cafés that didn't allow smoking on their premises, and this was way before the total ban came into place. I would instantly dismiss anyone's suggestions that I could lead a much healthier lifestyle without cigarettes. I dug my heels in firmly, even making sure I smoked double my usual quota on National No Smoking Day.

'I'm glad the governments have got nothing else better to do than waste money on no smoking campaigns,' I'd say. 'I will pack up when I am good and ready, and not before!'

I absolutely hated the idea of being told what to do. I still feel that way to a certain extent, and I am in no doubt that there are many more who feel exactly the same way as I do. But I can almost guarantee that the only way to inspire others successfully is through understanding, diplomacy and love.

Through my own repetitive mistakes, I realise that being hateful towards the perpetrators of unjust behaviour is not the answer. Neither is being judgemental towards others' opinions and lifestyles, without understanding their journey or seeing both sides of an argument.

Shouting at the TV has been a general hobby of mine in the past, usually when I decide to catch up with the news. But now I grimace with disappointment whenever I spot myself getting drawn into a heated debate, understanding that it isn't just the presenter or interviewer getting wound up, but me too. Thankfully, though, the time I spend hurling cross words at my 42-inch flat screen TV are becoming a lot less frequent. That's not because my values have changed or diminished in any way, but quite the opposite. I just know now that these types of negative emotions do not help any situation.

We can never be at peace with ourselves until we appreciate our connection to everyone – and that includes strangers and people we dislike, as well as family and friends.

Use social media smartly.

Sharing things on social media could be the first step in helping to create a better world. But unfortunately, sometimes you can get entangled in a web of negativity. Sometimes it's driven by your own personal drama or someone else's.

The success of my last few charity events is down to the vast number of networking opportunities that the internet has opened up for me. It's been incredibly fulfilling to help raise the profiles of other charities and business pages too. Due to my background in sales and marketing, I've found it quite easy to draw people's attention to whatever is being promoted.

Social media is now a major platform for businesses of all sizes, and since I launched A Compassionate Voice in September 2013, my profile has grown substantially. It took over 12 months before my official Facebook page gained 1,000 followers. And although I was constantly besieged by companies offering me popularity by purchase, I was determined that authenticity was the only way forward for ACV.

The first 1,000 followers seemed to take forever, but I was never tempted to paint a rosier picture by buying 20,000 batches of Facebook or Twitter followers. If I didn't think my talent – coupled with gritty determination – couldn't attract these numbers realistically, then surely, I had no faith in what I was doing.

So, with a budgeted amount of advertising to reach a wider market, I have grown my social media presence. I was over the moon every time the page reached its next thousand followers. It's incredibly fulfilling knowing that I am constantly influencing a growing audience through my creativity – especially since it's all derived from hard work, patience and sincerity.

The right image will always speak volumes, but the words we write are key.

I cringe when I remember some of my statuses during my dark and troubled days. Did I really believe people were interested in the fact that I was going to take an incredibly long soak in a bath, surrounded by scented candles? I doubt it, but it did spark the imagination of some members of the opposite sex, who were caught up in a virtual reality that I'd scripted for myself. I often wondered why I was littered with friend requests from single men, who were obviously using social media as a dating arena. In hindsight, it was hardly surprising – documenting my every movement, meal, thought and emotion was bound to generate some curiosity.

We can definitely learn a lot about ourselves through our social media profiles. Our general view of the world tends to reflect our emotions, weaknesses and innermost fears. It can certainly be an eye opener to scroll through old postings, and one of the easiest ways to understand someone else's present state of mind is to view their personal timeline too.

One problem with social media is that it's hard to read tone in words, and messages can often be misconstrued, which is why I created a few online rules to adhere to. Of course, I don't always get it right, but having been the victim of some unsavoury postings over recent years – and either through retaliation or anger, the composer of a few unjustified Facebook statuses too – I now follow these three simple guidelines:

1. Never post on social media after drinking alcohol.

2. Never publicly post anything in anger or retaliation.

3. Always think first and read through posts to ensure they cannot be misread or misinterpreted.

There is nothing brave about sitting behind a keypad and telling someone exactly how you feel. It's so much easier to write cutting remarks and ignore your conscience when you're facing a PC or mobile screen rather than your intended victim, especially when those comments are triggered by frustration, envy, spite or anger.

Besides, would you seriously say all those things to someone if you were looking them in the eye? Is it absolutely necessary to tell the world about your outrage, or could the problem be discussed privately? Although a status or update is quite easy to delete, once you have published your opinion, someone can always capture the words and remember them. Maybe this isn't always such a serious problem, but it is if it changes that person's perception of who you are.

No matter how awful, unjust, or hopeless the situation may seem, you should always give yourself a few moments. Take some deep breaths and ask yourself several questions before publishing:

1. What is the most probable outcome?

2. Is that honestly the outcome you I want to achieve?

3. Will it change your present circumstances, or are you just letting off steam?

It's always healthy to consider whether the post is helping in some way or if it's just keeping the raging fire of your hatred burning. Giving yourself time to contemplate the options is not going to hurt your immediate situation – quite the opposite! Acting on impulse, particularly if you're swayed by anger, will often shut down productive dialogue.

Just like in meditation – or any regular positive practice – the more you consider your actions, the easier it becomes to control your emotions. With a balanced mind, you can analyse difficulties from a much broader perspective and consider the different viewpoints.

If you can take this stance, leading the way for others to follow, the possibility of harmony is so much greater.

We all make mistakes.

We must be the change we wish to see in the world first, because without doubt it is far better to practise what we preach. But we should *inspire* others rather than preach to them, particularly if our own journeys have not always been whiter than white.

I have helped vulnerable children for years and have been a lover of animals all my life. I hate to see any living being come to harm or get treated cruelly. But like everyone else, I am human. And that definitely spells not perfect.

Although I am now a vegetarian, I toyed with the idea for years before finally deciding to embrace the change. Although I was never a huge meat eater, it was still a part of my diet for a while. And I have probably bought clothes that children from deprived countries stitched together for nothing more than food as payment. I've worn cosmetics tested on animals too.

At 20 years old I regrettably bought a second-hand fur coat. It reeked of mothballs and was a size 22, making it far too big and much too long for my figure. It was only in my wardrobe for a short while, because even though I tried to convince myself that the animal had probably died years ago, it still didn't feel right.

What I am trying to say is that we're all probably guilty of making choices for pleasure, without thinking first about the consequences. It's not because we consciously think *sod the vulnerable, sod child labour and sod other living beings.* It's because most of the time we make decisions unconsciously. We also live in a world that has tried to hide the sinister truth – the truth about war and famine in far off places, sexual abuse, what's in our food, and how our clothes and other commodities are being manufactured. We're exposed to lies about the millions of animals exploited, driven to extinction, stolen from their habitats and killed so that manufacturers and building companies can take over their homes. We're a humane population, but we've been cleverly desensitised into thinking that what is happening in our world today is the only way.

Taking all this into account, there is plenty of scope for people to change. But it needs to happen through encouragement, not condemnation!

We all make mistakes – sometimes grave ones – but that doesn't mean we can't change, or that we are bad people.

It is far too easy to criticise someone without first listening to their story. This book has given a clear indication of my past errors, and that's why I'm reluctant to condemn anyone else.

Smile at your blunders and learn an important lesson from them. This will then enable you to move through every stage of your existence with very little to fear.

The right education is key.

Without a shadow of a doubt, school education plays a huge role in moulding who we become. As babies and children we are shaped by our parents, families and teachers. But so often we repress our deepest desires and talents through a fear of not fitting into society.

'This is how it's always been!' is often the answer when someone dares to question age old traditions. Generation after generation passes down beliefs and teachings to children, some of which perhaps no longer serve the world we live in today.

Our world seems increasingly driven by consumerism, and yet we're not always made fully aware of what lies ahead when we're in school. While I believe that Maths, English, Science, History and geography understandably need to be part of the curriculum, there also has to be much more emphasis placed on the importance of connection between people.

We're told that if we study hard enough at school and leave with qualifications, that will steer us along the right course. And if the educational system's targets have been achieved, it's considered a job well done. But there is so much more that needs to be done.

We are all guilty from a lack of judgement sometimes. We are all prone to making irresponsible decisions too, especially in our younger years. Immaturity clouds our vision, because we think we know it all and yet we understand so little. But if there are to be any positive changes in this world, young minds must also learn about difference – and that includes skin colour, disability, mental illness, religion, and differences in ability and talent.

We need to understand at an early age that contrast shapes the planet. No life is any more or less important than another.

Ideally lessons should also include mindfulness, meditation, how to handle finance, and health in body and mind. All are key ingredients to good wellbeing; each are of paramount importance for a stable, more fulfilling life. Most significant of all, schools must encourage compassion and kindness, not only towards other living beings, but regarding ourselves too.

We need more mental health awareness.

The physical symptoms for someone suffering mental illness can be profound. But unlike a deep wound or a broken leg, often mental illness can be invisible. This makes it easy for a victim of this terrible disease to give the impression that they are absolutely fine. But it is behind closed doors when the affliction tends to kick in – when no one is looking.

This is the reason we find it so hard to believe when we hear that celebrities – who seem to have everything – are battling with the illness. Mental illness is so often a continual *inner* suffering.

Depression played me in a very similar way, so I completely understand why it isn't always detected by others until it is far too late.

Since my first serious bout of depression, acceptance and understanding of mental health issues has greatly improved. But there is still a long way to go. We can help to turn this around, with an openness and willingness to stand together as one voice. With a lot of hard work we can finally kick out the shame attached to the illness.

Ease the pressure you put on yourself.

I advocate being busy; I have always thrived if there is plenty to do. But stress is the number one trigger for most illness, and according to several surveys it is activated by two key factors: work and money.

Work and money were the two prime contributors to my own poor mental health, both of which I now sensibly manage. This allows me to maintain a much more benevolent and healthier lifestyle.

I believe that people's interest in my story is because my past experiences lift the lid on the toxic effects that society can have on people's lives. It highlights the huge pressure we put on ourselves, as we tirelessly strive to live out the perfect lifestyles seen in magazines, adverts and media.

We should have high standards, hopes and aspirations. But we lose many precious moments by continually reaching for the stars – without appreciating what is already available to us.

Status, wealth and possessions are not everything.

It's not easy to be authentic in a world where even becoming second in a race is never quite good enough. But the only steps I will now consider taking in my present career are the ones that feel right in my heart. Being the best at what you do isn't such a bad thing, but if we stay entrenched in the belief that wealth and possessions define a person's value, then we'll continue to breed a selfishness that overshadows compassion and kindness towards others.

All around the world there are many who are suffering and barely able to make ends meet. Some are living on the streets without homes, and some children go without food. How many winners can there be in a world like this? How many people have to suffer because of this possession-led mentality?

How different could the world be if we fed our own creativity and listened to our true selves, instead of constantly trying to impress others through possessions, status and wealth?

Humanity's ongoing pursuit of material things seems to derive from the ideology that superficial things are intrinsic to a perfect life. Using my own personal delusions as examples in this book, I have tried to show that happiness reliant on external things is like living on shaky ground. Love yourself for who you truly are today – not tomorrow or in two months' time, when you've lost weight, found a partner, or bought the perfect house – and then you'll be truly happy.

Teamwork is essential – when done for the right reasons.

I strongly believe that in order to achieve anything, you must put the hard work in yourself.

We are, however, social beings, and relationships can be beneficial to everyone concerned. Teamwork is essential – not just within business, but within life itself. I do believe, though, that we should never use others purely for their abilities and nothing else.

I have known lots of people who could have lifted me into higher circles or dug me out of my debt and depression hellhole. But I have never relied on anyone purely to elevate myself or help me climb the social ladder – not even friends.

The only exception to this personal rule has been when I have asked for help at my charity events. I would get on my hands and knees for donations and sponsorship.

I will always seek advice from people more learnt than myself, particularly if it's about a field I want to explore. This is exactly what I did when I spoke to Jools Holland, a musician and TV presenter who is a dear friend of mine. He put me in touch with William Sieghart, who founded National Poetry day in 1994. A British entrepreneur, publisher and poet, he spent a considerable amount of time chatting with me about the pitfalls I was likely to encounter within the literary world. I was especially appreciative of his poet's survival tips, using them as guidelines to strengthen S.M. Toni's business model.

No matter how high someone ranked – or how important they were within society – their power or lack of it was never my first priority.

The only time we stop loving is when we lose faith in ourselves. Mindfulness and meditation helps!

When making positive improvements in life, you have a duty to make sure you have the mental and physical wellbeing to cope with any knockbacks you might face. It doesn't matter how big or how small the goal may be, without first taking care of your wellbeing, you are not being fair to yourself. You must believe you are capable of achieving what it is you want when you actively set out to make those changes.

How many times do we hear stories about the knockbacks that highly talented artists, musicians and scientists face, only for them to finally come back and prove their doubters wrong?

You have the potential to deal with many circumstances effectively. You can even handle events that you're unable to control more positively by changing the way you feel about yourself. Having faith in your own capabilities shifts your perception, so that you are less likely to write off difficult situations or decisions. You will no longer automatically assume that a problem is hopeless.

I am confident that mindfulness and meditation helps you do this. It helps you assess incidents in a much broader context and makes your role in life far easier to understand.

For this reason, I feel even more convinced that mindfulness should be included in the school curriculum. I've experienced sensational health benefits in both my mind and body after just a few years of practice. But it's never too late to bring it into your life, especially if it encourages peace of mind, compassion and kindness.

People with true grit, determination, and a strong vision will not be put off by sceptics or dismissive people, because they have indelible hope. And if they hang on to this hope, they will always find a way.

CHAPTER 18

step outside the box

There is little I crave for these days, but although my bucket list has changed considerably over the past few years, I still have many hopes and dreams to fulfil. My top 10 goals clearly illustrate a change in my priorities.

A future vision is to create an ACV fundraising arm called A Compassionate Voice Foundation. My mind is bursting at the seams with ideas. Each concept is waiting desperately to be incorporated into exciting projects.

The charity will stay certain of its mission: to unite children with animals and nature. Children are the ambassadors of the future, so for me it's of utmost importance that we educate them about our connection to nature and other living things.

I understand that we all want different experiences. I am by no means a dream stealer, snatching people's hopes of enjoying their life to the full. We all want to live comfortable, happy, and healthy lives. Sometimes we hanker for what we believe to be the ideal home to live in, and aspire to careers in which we'll thrive the most. None of these wishes are a crime, if you're true to yourself.

But in this final chapter of the book, I don't think I can put enough emphasis on the importance of being true to ourselves, rather than living our lives like puppets, allowing our strings to be pulled by a multitude of different external forces. As sinister as this may sound, everyone is vulnerable to this type of manipulation, until we cut the strings and value our own capabilities, ideas, and decisions.

It is easy to scoff and tell yourself that you're always in complete control. But take some time to reflect on past events – good or bad. This will give you a clear indication as to whether you are truly the master of your own destiny.

My strings were almost certainly pulled by my psychiatrist when I was a young woman. His words pulled my strings for the next 30 years.

'No man will marry you looking like that. Men don't marry women like you!'

For years, my idea of the perfect home was a mansion-type house, with a walk-in wardrobe as big as an average master bedroom. For me, this was the most important feature: a large, mirrored room dedicated solely to my endless collection of designer clothes and shoes. It would have just about accommodated my incessant and incontrollable thirst for spending, but it would have been little more than a showcase of my gluttony, addiction, and mental health issues.

Over the past couple of years, though, my dream has been for a much humbler property, and now it's been realised. Mum's bungalow was in an idyllic location; it looked out onto fields and we often had garden visitors. But the problem was that our home was far too small, and it severely affected my writing. With nowhere to go to be alone with my creativity, I was having to spend money on small B&Bs. I needed to be able to sit in front of my laptop if I wanted to continue writing books, blogs, and verse, so the most important feature for a future home had to be an office.

And so, on 29th November 2016, Mum and I moved into a bigger house. We both fell in love with the bungalow instantly. It ticked all our boxes perfectly: it had the perfect extra room for my office and it was even near a country park. It almost felt as though our prayers had been answered.

We surprised both family and friends by our sudden decision to relocate. It all happened so quickly – no sooner had I returned from a trip to China than we were packing up and ordering a removal van.

But even though it was a switch into a new county, it hardly mattered. Moving house is supposed to be one of life's most stressful events, and our relocation didn't come without its frustrations and hold-ups. But even though I bore the brunt for my 79-year-old mum, I managed somehow to avoid any major anxiety hiccups.

The move came after I'd spent five arduous days trekking along, across, up, and down some of the remotest parts of the Great Wall of China. It had put an awful lot into perspective. Taking place in October 2016, it had been an almighty challenge to conquer. Regardless of all my personal hang-ups, I have never been scared to step outside the box, but it was probably one of the biggest endurance tests I have ever undertaken.

It had come about after I'd seen Jill Robinson, the founder of Animals Asia, speak in Birmingham during her visit to the UK in 2015. Jill had founded Animals Asia in 1998, five years after her encounter with a caged bear on a bile farm in southern China. This changed Jill's life forever, and that's when she'd vowed to put an end to bear bile farming. Since then the charity has rescued hundreds of moon bears from their tiny cages in China and Vietnam, many of whom have existed in this barbaric way for 15 years or more – simply for their bile.

Inspired by her passion and ethics, which resonated with me on every level, I knew immediately I wanted to help the charity.

So, on 12th October, I boarded an airbus from London's Heathrow airport for the 14-hour flight to Beijing. Being a nervous flier, the thought of this alone was stomach-churning, but the real endurance test was yet to come.

I had worked extremely hard to get fit for almost a year, but no amount of training could have fully prepared me for the punishing terrain I was about to face. It was a five-day trek to raise money and awareness for Animals Asia, and each individual hike lasted seven to eight hours. I'd almost accomplished the mission when, on the final day, my legs couldn't take any more. My feet – despite being in walking boots – seemed to take on a life of their own, skidding and stumbling over the loose stones. Each rock felt like Mount Everest as I positioned my walking poles to hoist myself upwards and forwards.

Looking ahead and seeing how far I still had left to go, I burst into tears. Enough was enough.

I had overcome so much during those past five days, but I knew it was time to quit. With no shame, I stepped away from the climb. I didn't make it to the highest point of the trek, but I savoured all that I had mastered during the challenge. I celebrated my new-found stamina in the face of fear. I rejoiced in the knowledge that my participation would raise awareness and money for Animals Asia's ongoing crusade.

Taking part in the Great Wall of China Trek Challenge was, for all intents and purposes, an unexpected event, one which had never been on my bucket list. But we really do have a minuscule time on this wonderful planet. Particularly as we grow older, the days seem to pass by so quickly. The months very swiftly blend into years, so it certainly makes sense to use our precious gift of life as wisely as we can.

Mother Earth is vast and diverse, and while we do well to experience as much of the world as we possibly can, its hidden treasures often stare us right in the face. Sometimes they beckon us from the most unexpected places. Sometimes they are as small as a warm gesture from a fellow human being, a beautiful landscape through a train window, or wildlife in a garden.

I now value these experiences far more than hoarding personal possessions. Maybe, deep down, I always did. We can treasure memories for a lifetime, but the novelty of new belongings diminishes very quickly, particularly in the 21st century when we are constantly encouraged to upgrade to a more up-to-date model.

The wardrobe in my new home is a standard size, but it's more than enough to cater for my needs. Mum and I are making fond memories in our new environment. I hope I am lucky enough to live out the rest of my life peacefully, happily, and with good health, but no matter when it is time for me to leave this world behind, I pray I will have fulfilled enough of my goals to recognise that there was a definite purpose to my own personal journey.

I may not have conformed to society's idea of "perfect" womanhood – I became neither a wife nor a mother. But for me, none of this matters any more. If I can help in whatever way I can to transform people's mindsets – to help create a kinder, more compassionate society – then my existence will have been worthwhile.

I have sympathy with anyone who is suffering from a mental health disorder, because we still have the task of trying to explain to people who don't have knowledge or experience just how torturous living with the illness can be. For over 30 years, depression and anxiety held me prisoner.

I'm not completely stupid. I have no misconceptions about making a full recovery. From time to time, depression still tries to swoop down on me, desperate to catch me unawares at any golden opportunity. But through my continued practice of daily meditation and mindfulness, I am able to stay in control and maintain the upper hand.

It hasn't been easy to tell a story that has travelled across three decades. It hasn't been easy writing about my life-changing experiences. But I believed the best place to start was at the beginning, which is exactly what I did. Retracing my steps from childhood to where I am now has enabled me to see what was hidden behind my own personal issues for many years. Hopefully it will help countless others to overcome their own particular hurdles too.

Stepping outside the box isn't just about bravery and expanding your comfort zones. It's about stepping away from routines and habits that dull your senses and hinder your progress in life. It's about recognising your potential and the opportunities you have already available to you. Of course, it is also about daring to lead the way, using the right temperament to empower others, and losing our fear of tapping into unchartered territory to resolve issues.

But, over and above all of this, it's about willingness to grow and learn.

Never expect too much too soon, though. Spending quality time establishing what truly makes you happy is a far better option than grasping frantically for solutions. Events, circumstances, and people don't always knit together as we would like, but as I have learnt in more ways than one, patience and tenacity will always produce the right results.

My deepest wish is for everyone who reads this book to be inspired enough to take action and create change. Not only for ourselves, but for others too. Persistence is key, but if we hold on to unwavering hope, listen to our hearts, and act purely from unconditional love, understanding, and compassion, there will always be a way through.

Reliance on material goods and wealth for happiness is most definitely the biggest humanitarian misconception of all. The idea that yearning for more and searching for perfection holds the key to an unproblematic lifestyle is just a fairy tale.

I was plagued by mental health issues, and a little retail therapy eventually became a habit. It ultimately turned into a shopping addiction. Just like any other addiction – drugs, gambling, alcoholism, food, work – it started to encroach on other areas of my life, finally leaving me with £50,000 worth of debt and almost nothing to my name.

Since stripping away all the materialism and consumerism from my life, I have found the real Sharon Bull. Writing, nature, kindness, and compassion have completely transformed my life.

I have finally fallen in love with who I am.

To find out more about Animals Asia please visit **www.animalsasia.org**

STRIPPED BARE

This is the story about me.
But what you might see
and recognise within me,
Is perhaps a part of you too?

Because you see, we can all look at each other
and think wow she's got it good,
Because you see, it's how we paint the picture
We must fit in, be understood,
We play our roles the best we can
to put a show on for one another,
And even though it's totally wrong
our true self we often smother,
We feel alone, we all compete
we search for praise and glory,
And when our life turns upside down,
We repeat the same sob story

Because you see, we can all look at each other
and think hey, he's looking good,
Because you see, it's how we paint the picture
We must fit in, be understood,
Our world is from perceptions,
We create images of who people are,
So, at any given moment
They can change from a hero, into a villain and then a star,
And perhaps we think we need them
And perhaps they feel the same,
But either way we are encouraged to always stay
one step ahead of the game,

Because do we really trust them
Our past issues tell us no,
But is it fair to base, compare
On what we really should let go,

What we see are our illusions,
And we all try to smother and cover
The vulnerable side we wish to hide
as we play charades with one another,

People look at me and see confident
They see relaxed and self-assured,
But behind this glint, behind this smile
I can tell you it's been a fraud,
Then others say she's glamorous
they must queue at least a mile,
Well here's a little secret
I've never once walked down the aisle,
And then they say "It's time to pray
because she hasn't married yet,"
But here's the thing, there is no ring
because we simply haven't met,
And then in the past, it's been eccentric
unhinged and slightly loopy,
Because I didn't blend in with the high-street mass
I couldn't be a fashion groupie,
And depression stank and I'd like to thank
The few who understood,
At times life's unkind, sometimes jinxed
But with inner strength it can turn good,

So, this is me stripped bare
Beneath the lipstick and underwear,
This is me exposed,
Determined and now transposed
from a darkened place to a place of light
And this I have to share,
Because whatever your plight, you can overwrite
When you're mindful and aware,

So, tell me are you happy
Tell me are you sad,

The chances are you're in-between
Maybe fearful, sometimes glad,
And perhaps an outside situation
has changed your inner mood,
But all you need, it comes from within
The rest is misconstrued,
And no one needs possession
Of others or of things,
Let go of hurt and grievances
It's amazing what this brings,

Because you see it's time we all loved one another
No matter what we see,
Because appearances are deceptive
I'm sure you will agree,
We put strangers in marked boxes
Create labels to identify,
Often based on our own personal principles
Our life's morals to satisfy,
But the influences are all around us
The media have their views,
Social sites can corrupt, distort things
And negativity is headline news,

But we cannot know how the next man feels
We should only hold out our hand,
Because if we share our love, show compassion
This will help us to understand,
Because you see it's time, we all loved one another
and leave judgement by the door,
And although it's me I've let you see
I'm almost certain you'll see more!

©Sharon Bull
www.acompassionatevoice.co.uk

ACKNOWLEDGEMENTS

This book would never have been written without the continued support from loyal friends and family. My appreciation and thanks go out to every one of you for believing in what I have been trying to achieve over the past five years. Extra special thanks go to: my mum, who without a shadow of a doubt has been my guardian angel, particularly during my darkest hours; my dear departed father, who has always been my strength since I was a little girl, which made it more difficult when he parted from this world in 2003; my younger brother Paul, his wife Joanne and my beautiful nephew Jude; my cousin Sandy, my two dearest friends Marie and Margaret, and my beautiful pet cat Maddie.

I have met many inspirational people along the way, some who have become great friends too. I would like to thank Alan Dolman, the first person to believe I could make something of myself; Squeeze, for unknowingly encouraging me to make it happen, and Paul Davies, my mentor for finally connecting all the dots. I would also like to thank Trigger and the team for helping to bring this book together so beautifully, giving myself and other authors the opportunity to raise awareness of mental health issues through our own personal stories.

To everyone who has given me both the encouragement and strength to continue along this path, my gratitude is eternal.

Sharon Bull

www.acompassionatevoice.co.uk

If you found this book interesting ...
why not read this next?

Stress In The City
Playing My Way Out Of Depression

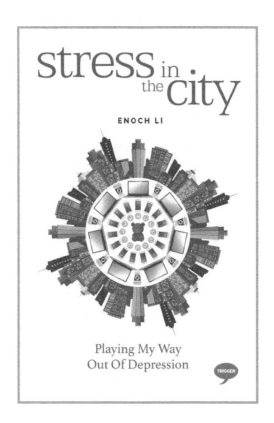

Stress in the City is a fascinating, information-packed self-help memoir, tackling the subjects of corporate pressure, depression and the benefits of playfulness within the recovery process.

**If you found this book interesting ...
why not read this next?**

Depression In A Digital Age

The Highs and Lows of Perfectionism

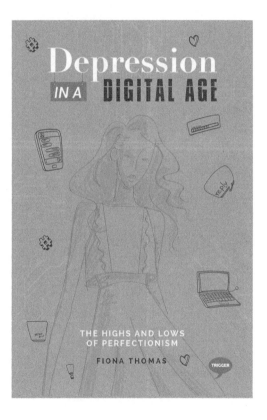

Depression in a Digital Age traces the journey of a young woman's
search for perfection in a world filled with filters.

**If you found this book interesting ...
why not read this next?**

Shiny Happy Person

Finding The Sun Between Clouds of Depression

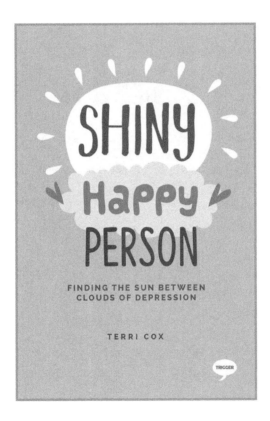

Shiny Happy Person is one young woman's story of
how she overcame The Judge, her poisonous inner critic, and
found freedom from her depression and anxiety.

the *Shaw* **mind**
FOUNDATION

Creating hope for children,
adults and families

Sign up to our charity, The Shaw Mind Foundation
www.shawmindfoundation.org
and keep in touch with us; we would love to hear
from you.

*We aim to end the suffering and despair caused by mental
health issues. Our goal is to make help and support available
for every single person in society, from all walks of life. We will
never stop offering hope. These are our promises.*

www.triggerpublishing.com

Trigger is a publishing house devoted to opening conversations about mental health. We tell the stories of people who have suffered from mental illnesses and recovered, so that others may learn from them.

Adam Shaw is a worldwide mental health advocate and philanthropist. Now in recovery from mental health issues, he is committed to helping others suffering from debilitating mental health issues through the global charity he co-founded, The Shaw Mind Foundation. www.shawmindfoundation.org

Lauren Callaghan (CPsychol, PGDipClinPsych, PgCert, MA (hons), LLB (hons), BA), born and educated in New Zealand, is an innovative industry-leading psychologist based in London, United Kingdom. Lauren has worked with children and young people, and their families, in a number of clinical settings providing evidence based treatments for a range of illnesses, including anxiety and obsessional problems. She was a psychologist at the specialist national treatment centres for severe obsessional problems in the UK and is renowned as an expert in the field of mental health, recognised for diagnosing and successfully treating OCD and anxiety related illnesses in particular. In addition to appearing as a treating clinician in the critically acclaimed and BAFTA award-winning documentary *Bedlam*, Lauren is a frequent guest speaker on mental health conditions in the media and at academic conferences. Lauren also acts as a guest lecturer and honorary researcher at the Institute of Psychiatry Kings College, UCL.

Please visit the link below:

www.triggerpublishing.com

Join us and follow us...

@triggerpub

Search for us on Facebook